Word

The Bible Day by Day
January–April 2009

HODDER &
STOUGHTON

Unless indicated otherwise, Scripture quotations are taken from the
Holy Bible, New International Version.
Copyright © 1973, 1978, 1984 by International Bible Society.
Used by permission. All rights reserved.

First published in Great Britain in 2009 by Hodder & Stoughton
An Hachette Livre UK company

A CIP catalogue record for this title is available from the British Library

ISBN 978 0 340 97937 2

Typeset in Minion by Avon DataSet Ltd, Bidford on Avon, Warwickshire

Printed and bound in Great Britain
by Clays Ltd, St Ives plc

Hodder & Stoughton policy is to use papers that are natural, renewable
and recyclable products and made from wood grown in sustainable forests.
The logging and manufacturing processes are expected to conform to the
environmental regulations of the country of origin.

Hodder & Stoughton Ltd
338 Euston Road
London NW1 3BH

www.hodderfaith.com

Contents

From the writer of *Words of Life* v

Beginning Again 1
1 January–14 February

Belief in Action 48
The Epistle of James
16–28 February

Partnerships in Ministry 63
Guest writers Lieutenant-Colonels Richard and Janet Munn
2–28 March

In Galilee 92
Readings from Matthew's Gospel
30 March–23 April

Open Wide the Windows 118
24–30 April

Sundays

In line with the custom of treating Sunday readings differently from those for the other days of the week, most of the Sunday readings in this edition continue a recent *Words of Life* pattern, employing verse. As Scripture counsels: 'Speak to one another with psalms, hymns and spiritual songs' (Ephesians 5:19).

From the writer of *Words of Life*

According to author Gail Kislevitz, no matter how many marathons people run, they always remember their first. Her *First Marathons* is a collection of such stories. Some recall the feeling of running through a tunnel of people, the encouragement from the crowd when 'hitting the wall' or the elation of finishing the course.

Writing my first edition of *Words of Life* has been a marathon of sorts. This edition is coming to the finish line five months after the assignment began. Possibly writing for university courses and The Salvation Army's Literary Department in New York unwittingly conditioned me for the task.

I join others who have participated in this unique marathon. I acknowledge words of encouragement and invaluable promises of prayer support from friends and colleagues. I treasure the wise advice from the previous three marathon writers of *Words of Life*. I am grateful for the assistance and guidance of my International Headquarters coaches, Majors Charles King and Trevor Howes, as they've edited my contributions and worked with our partners at joint-publisher Hodder & Stoughton. Happily we have all survived the race. Lieutenant-Colonels Richard and Janet Munn were selected as guest writers for this edition prior to my assignment as writer and I am grateful for their contributions as well.

This edition of *Words of Life* runs through varied terrain. We start in Genesis, continue with James, add a special loop through 'partners in ministry', keep on with Matthew (including through Holy Week) and finish with thoughts about windows.

Most of all, I thank God for his sustaining grace. All Christians are marathon runners of sorts. Happily, God knows our frames and tailors the pace of the race. With his help we continue to run and to encourage each other.

Evelyn Merriam
New York, USA

Abbreviations

AB	The Amplified Bible. Copyright © 1965 Zondervan.
DT	Darby Translation.
JBP	*The New Testament in Modern English*, J. B. Phillips, Geoffrey Bless. © J. B. Phillips, 1958, 1959, 1960, 1972. HarperCollins Publishers.
JMT	James Moffatt Translation. © 1922, 1924, 1925, 1926, 1935. HarperCollins Publishers.
KJV	King James Bible (Authorised Version).
MSG	*The Message*, Eugene H. Peterson. © 1993, 1994, 1995, 1996, 2000, 2001, 2002. Used by permission of NavPress Publishing Group.
NKJV	New King James Bible®. Copyright © 1982 by Thomas Nelson, Inc. Used by permission. All rights reserved.
SASB	*The Song Book of The Salvation Army*. Copyright © 1986 The General of The Salvation Army.
TNIV	Today's New International Version. Copyright © 2004 by International Bible Society. Used by permission of Hodder & Stoughton Publishers, an Hachette Livre UK company. All rights reserved. 'TNIV' is a registered trademark of International Bible Society.
WNT	Wesley New Testament.

Beginning Again

When Michelangelo was commissioned to paint the Sistine Chapel, he lived with the theme of creation and his daily portrayal of it for several years. We spend some of the early days of this new year with the story of creation. When God spoke, his will was expressed by his Word and executed by his Spirit in orderly progression. What parts of God's creation, whether in delicate microcosm or vast space, strikes awe in your spirit? Could we view the universe as a temple of sorts in which God's creation praises him? In his *Advancement of Learning*, Francis Bacon urged endless study in both the book of God's Word and the book of God's work (creation).

We start with Genesis, a cornerstone in the historical foundation of the record of God and humankind. Martin Luther said, 'There is nothing more beautiful than the book of Genesis, and nothing more useful. It is certainly the foundation of the whole of Scripture.'

Genesis is placed first in the Bible not because it is the oldest book, but because of its subject matter. Whether meaning 'origin' (Greek) or 'in the beginning' (Hebrew), we understand that the first chapters deal with the essential start to our world, as well as with the start to monotheism, humankind, encounters with sin and a hope of salvation. Since we're bundled with them in the human condition, we find that we resonate with people who faced choices and changes in life across generations and eras – all the way back to the beginning. We will pause after introducing Abraham.

When we occasionally use the same Scripture passage for more than one day, you may want to consider reading it from different versions.

On Sundays we will continue a recent *Words of Life* pattern, employing verse. As Scripture counsels: 'Speak to one another with psalms, hymns and spiritual songs. Sing and make music in your heart to the Lord, always giving thanks to God the Father for everything, in the name of our Lord Jesus Christ' (Ephesians 5:19, 20). Whether our windows frame balmy summer or bleak winter scenes at the start of a new year, on Sundays we will let songwriters and psalmists turn our grateful hearts toward the Creator of our world.

New Things

' "See, I am doing a new thing! Now it springs up; do you not perceive it?
I am making a way in the desert and streams in the wasteland" ' (v. 19).

Whether you're an occasional or avid reader, welcome to *Words of Life* for the new year, 2009. Each slim edition offers a means to meet together over brief, fresh thoughts on timeless Bible truths. A new year is important for all of us, but it's especially significant in certain parts of the world. Do you start the year with all your debts paid, a thoroughly clean house, a fresh haircut and a week of celebration with specially prepared traditional foods? Some do.

This month, *Words of Life* starts the year with a new writer. Do new things entice you or give you pause? When I open something new, sometimes I can't start to use it immediately. Maybe I want the newness to last or just need time to adjust to a new thing. If reading *Words of Life* is new to you, you may be interested to know of some ways it can be helpful.

Some readers use it for daily personal devotions, some as a devotional supplement. Some read it together with others in their household. A Japanese pastor used it as tool for Christian growth in his church and kept track of how many members read it. Some readers have read *Words of Life* or its predecessor, *The Soldier's Armoury*, for decades. Some catalogue the editions in their library. Others pass on their copies or keep just a few salient pages.

Perhaps you'll tell us how you use it. Do you read the portions daily or several at once? Do you read the full Bible passage or just the key verse and devotional thought? Is it your chief daily Bible teaching or a supplement to other helps?

As someone has suggested, more than mastering biblical passages, we need to permit the Bible to *read* us. If we allow that to happen we will discover that we are known. Then in light of the Word, we can ask the Spirit to change our hearts. Let's pray that the Lord will do a new thing in us this year as we meet at his Word!

———

To pray:

Pray for hearts open to both new and old treasures from the Word.

Watching over His Word

'The word of the LORD came to me: "What do you see, Jeremiah?" "I see the branch of an almond tree," I replied. The LORD said to me, "You have seen correctly, for I am watching to see that my word is fulfilled"' (vv. 11, 12).

Janus, the two-headed Roman mythological figure who looked both backward and forward, gives January its name. We too look both ways at the outset of *Words of Life* as we begin January 2009.

I've read previous editions with appreciation. Each author brought a different style and set of life experiences to the challenge of writing *Words of Life*. Commissioner Harry Read, Major Barbara Sampson and Retired General John Gowans have been our gifted guides for a generation and we are grateful to them. General Gowans's verse sang scriptural truth into our hearts over the years. His recent contributions were a refreshing visit with him and the Word.

When I was given the opportunity of being the next writer, I sought the Lord's assurance. He spoke to me through what he said to Jeremiah at the outset of the prophet's own daunting task (1:1–12). Among other things, the Lord used object lessons to instruct his modest spokesman. In verse 11 he showed Jeremiah the branch of an almond tree. Trees such as the almond that blossom in late winter can symbolise hope – the hope of spring and the hope for fruit.

The almond branch Jeremiah saw also symbolised alertness and activity – watchfulness. The Lord said he is similarly watchful over his Word to perform it. We can proceed in that confidence as we listen for a word from the Lord.

We face the new year together trusting that God's Spirit will continue to speak hope and challenge to our hearts through his Word. We look both back to God's promises kept and ahead to those yet to be fulfilled, and affirm with a one-time General of The Salvation Army, Arnold Brown:

> I believe in God the Father,
> I believe in God the Son;
> I believe in the Holy Spirit,
> Blessèd Godhead, Three in One;
> I believe in a full salvation,
> In redemption through the blood;
> I believe I'll receive a crown of life,
> When I hear the Lord's: Well done.
> (*SASB* 222)

In the Beginning

'In the beginning God created the heavens and the earth' (v. 1).

Thousands watched the multimedia presentation *In the Beginning* as it depicted the creation story on stage. The drama engulfed the audience in light, colour, music, spinning planets, gliding angels, real animals and more, and brought to life what *might* have happened at creation.

Theories about the origins of the earth and its inhabitants continue to change. (Didn't it seem strange when Pluto was declassified as a planet?) Although interesting and inspiring, neither the stage nor scientific theory offers heart-staying certainty. While true science may fill in some of the details and art may stir our imaginations, the Word of the Lord is our reliable basis for spiritual truth: 'For everything that was written in the past was written to teach us, so that through endurance and the encouragement of the Scriptures we might have hope' (Romans 15:4).

J. Sidlow Baxter suggests there was a gap in time between the first two verses of Genesis. In that case, the six days of Genesis 1:2–31 describe a new beginning, after the initial vast act described in verse 1. More importantly, whenever and wherever the beginning was, God in completeness (tri-unity) was there beforehand and the initiative for creation was his alone.

He chooses to reveal something of himself to us through the creation story. 'For since the creation of the world God's invisible qualities – his eternal power and divine nature – have been clearly seen, being understood from what has been made, so that men are without excuse' (Romans 1:20).

Writer Philip Yancey said that reading Genesis while in the mountains instead of the city gave it a different tone and gave him a different perspective. Where are you reading Genesis? Take time today to appreciate something God created.

Another book of the Bible starts with the same words as Genesis and assures us that our Saviour, the living Word, is our Creator: 'In the beginning was the Word, and the Word was with God, and the Word was God. He was with God in the beginning. Through him all things were made; without him nothing was made that has been made' (John 1:1–3). Hallelujah!

Psalm of Creation

Genesis 1:1–2:3 has been called a creation hymn. Could Psalm 148 be in the same category? The psalmist urges us with all of creation to praise the Lord. As we do, let's also consider how we can be better stewards of creation.

Praise the LORD.

Praise the LORD from the heavens,
praise him in the heights above.
Praise him, all his angels,
praise him, all his heavenly hosts.
Praise him, sun and moon,
praise him, all you shining stars.
Praise him, you highest heavens
and you waters above the skies.
Let them praise the name of the LORD,
for he commanded and they were created.
He set them in place for ever and ever;
he gave a decree that will never pass away.

Praise the LORD from the earth,
you great sea creatures and all ocean depths,
lightning and hail, snow and clouds,
stormy winds that do his bidding,
you mountains and all hills,
fruit trees and all cedars,
wild animals and all cattle,
small creatures and flying birds,
kings of the earth and all nations,
you princes and all rulers on earth,
young men and maidens,
old men and children.

Let them praise the name of the LORD,
for his name alone is exalted;
his splendour is above the earth and the heavens.
He has raised up for his people a horn,
the praise of all his saints,
of Israel, the people close to his heart.

Praise the LORD.

First Light

'God called the light "day", and the darkness he called "night". And there
was evening, and there was morning – the first day' (v. 5).

The opening verses of Genesis move the account from the general to the specific. God's Spirit hovered over the dark nebulous deep. God said 'light' and light appeared. God started his extravaganza of creation with light. That is how essential it is to our universe and our world, to us, to life. We notice the difference in the length of days when our segment of the globe tilts even slightly toward or away from the sun. With that change the seasons shift and we have to accommodate our daily lives to the change by what we wear and how much fuel we use.

When the norm is radically changed the contrast is undeniable. Imagine a dark nebulous deep becoming radiant with light. In preparation for light, the earth was swathed by the Spirit of God (*Elohim*). In our lives too, his Spirit hovered over us when all was murky until Jesus, the Light of the World, penetrated our hearts: 'For God, who said, "Let light shine out of darkness," made his light shine in our hearts to give us the light of the knowledge of the glory of God in the face of Christ' (2 Corinthians 4:6).

William Hawley's verse reminds us:

> A light came out of darkness;
> No light, no hope had we,
> Till Jesus came from Heaven
> Our light and hope to be.
> Oh, as I read the story
> From birth to dying cry,
> A longing fills my bosom
> To meet him by and by.

Do you remember when the light of the gospel first warmed your heart? Thank the Lord for that first day of the whole new world he created in you and ask him to alert you to opportunities to 'declare the praises of him who called you out of darkness into his wonderful light' (1 Peter 2:9).

More Light

'And God said, "Let there be light," and there was light' (v. 3).

Light we can see isn't all there is of light. We know of infrared light and ultraviolet light and there are other parts of light undetectable to the human eye. But even the spectrum of light we can see is marvellous. Aside from the practical value of light, artists are always attuned to light and its effects.

Museums sometimes feature painters of light. An art museum devoted a whole exhibition to light itself. Its premise was that since light is so available today we don't notice it. But in earlier centuries darkness limited people's lives. There was only daylight, moonlight, firelight and lamplight. So when discoveries about light transformed life, some artists made the new experience of light itself into a subject and a medium for art.

Not only has God created light and given us spiritual light, but the Bible says God *is* light. Just as artists have not only enjoyed the benefits of light but turned to it as a worthwhile subject itself, we can focus on God as our light: 'This is the message we have heard from him and declare to you: God is light; in him there is no darkness at all' (1 John 1:5). 'Every good and perfect gift is from above, coming down from the Father of the heavenly lights, who does not change like shifting shadows' (James 1:17). In heaven, 'No one will need lamplight or sunlight. The shining of God, the Master, is all the light anyone needs' (Revelation 22:5b, *MSG*).

Jesus came into the darkness, not simply to bring light or to reveal the way through the darkness, or to reveal who God is and what God is like; Christ entered the world to claim it, redeem it and become one with it, not only as light, but also to share grace and truth with all who will receive him. Lines from Joseph Mohr's Christmas carol come to mind:

> Silent night! Holy night!
> Son of God, love's pure light,
> Radiant beams from thy holy face,
> With the dawn of redeeming grace,
> Jesus Lord at thy birth.

Water Everywhere

'God called the dry ground "land", and the gathered waters he called "seas". And God saw that it was good' (v. 10).

In how many ways have you used water today? We have a natural connection with water. It's a major component of our bodies and essential to our existence and health. I'm especially grateful for water for baths and pots of tea. As a child, the first book I borrowed from the public library was about water. How much water a dripping tap could waste in a day impressed me. Now I know that such a seemingly trivial thing, if multiplied, can affect many.

Lack of drinkable water has gained global attention. To increase awareness and action on behalf of the more than one billion people who live without safe drinking water, the United Nations has designated an annual World Water Day. Widespread droughts have underscored the issue and accelerated efforts to desalinate sea water. Perhaps you've supported The Salvation Army's efforts to fund new wells in various countries.

When God gathered the waters as seas, he said it was good and approved it (as he had light on day one and the sky on day two). Two thirds of our world is water. The interconnected oceans are fed by the rivers, streams and springs that extend far inland.

Jesus calls us to the spiritual water he alone offers, a perpetual eternal spring of life that can flow from us to others (John 7: 37, 38). Do you know that refreshment, and its overflow? It hinges on faith in Jesus and a willingness to continue to be an available clear conduit for his Spirit. We pray with a verse from hymnwriter Mary Susan Edgar:

> God who touchest earth with beauty,
> Make my heart anew;
> With thy Spirit recreate me
> Pure and strong and true.
> Like the springs of running waters
> Make me crystal pure;
> Like thy rocks of towering grandeur,
> Make me strong and sure.

Take time today to consider the value of both spiritual and physical water. In what ways can we help to bring both types to others?

Biosphere

'Then God said, "Let the land produce vegetation: seed-bearing plants and trees on the land that bear fruit with seed in it, according to their various kinds." And it was so' (v. 11).

Do you enjoy growing things? House plants? Flowers? Vegetables? Fruit trees? A blooming plant indoors in winter suggests the warmth of spring. On the first and second days of creation God commanded, something appeared, and he named what he had made. On the third day God ordered land and sea to separate, then directed earth to assist him and bring forth plants and trees. From the beginning, life rests on and responds to God's creative, orderly word. The plan for plants to contain seed and fruit that would perpetuate the original species is brilliant.

Vegetation is seen in many forms around our biodiverse planet. Photographs of plants quite unlike those that grow in our neighbourhoods amaze us. Climate-controlled botanical gardens offer an even closer glimpse of some of the wonders of the flora our Creator envisioned. Certain plants have been found to contain medicinal qualities (for example, aspirin comes from the willow tree). Others hold valuable antioxidants. Some are part of our daily diet. We need their nutrients for our bodies as we need the Word for our spirits. 'Man does not live on bread alone, but on every word that comes from the mouth of God' (Matthew 4:4).

In his parables Jesus frequently refers to things that grow (seeds, trees, vines, grain), knowing we all relate to nature and natural laws. Paul also uses growth metaphors. In Ephesians 3:17–19 he prays that, as Christ dwells in our hearts, we will be rooted and grounded in love, know the love of Christ and be filled with the fullness of God. In the next chapter Paul speaks of growing up into Christ.

To ponder and to pray:

We all depend on what someone else grows. Consider buying some locally grown produce and exploring Fairtrade products. Pray for those who work in the fields and orchards – their own or others' – to tend and harvest what we eat.

Luminaries

*'God made two great lights – the greater light to govern the day and
the lesser light to govern the night. He also made the stars' (v. 16).*

God calls forth two great lights that, although they are not named, we infer to
be our sun and moon (not naming them may have been to downplay the
then prevalent ancient pagan worship of the sun and moon). God sets them in
place to give light on the earth in a habitual day and night pattern.

Humankind has been fascinated for centuries with the placement and
movement of the heavenly bodies and to an extent has measured, analysed and
explored them. Before the invention of clocks, calendar, compass or longitude we
marked the passing time and charted our courses by the sun, moon and stars'
predictable patterns. Human activity has always been closely linked to nature's
cycles and consequently to these heavenly markers of time and seasons.

We know now of global warming, but what of global dimming? Scientists say
more particles in the air are screening out the sunlight we need. Light gives
warmth and stimulates growth. We need light to see physically and spiritually. The
psalmist David sings: 'For with you is the fountain of life; in your light we see light'
(Psalm 36:9).

We need light to find the way. The words of another psalm plead with God:
'Send forth your light and your truth, let them guide me; let them bring me to
your holy mountain, to the place where you dwell' (Psalm 43:3). Salvation Army
songwriter Ruth Tracy puts it this way:

> Send out thy light, let it lead me,
> Bring me to thy holy hill;
> When from all sin thou hast freed me,
> I shall delight in thy will.
> Jesus, thy wounding is tender,
> Kind is the light that reveals,
> Waiting until I surrender,
> Pouring the balm then that heals.
> (*SASB* 457)

Perhaps as we see the sun, moon or stars this week they will remind us of their
Maker and of the light he offers us.

Abundance in Sea and Sky

'God blessed them and said, "Be fruitful and increase in number and fill the water in the seas, and let the birds increase on the earth"' (v. 22).

A relation of mine in New England feeds a variety of birds that visit her area and regularly sees exquisite humming-birds, noisy jays, magnificent raptors and determined woodpeckers, as well as common garden visitors. Whether we have such a neighbour, visit an aviary or enjoy nature magazines or television programmes, many of us delight in the superb design of birds and their ability to fly.

At God's command water teemed with fish and sea creatures and the sky with birds. Imagine the sound of rushing wings in the air above and splashing in the waters below – reminiscent of scenes from *Winged Migration* or *The March of the Penguins*. This part of the Creator's plan involved the creatures' participation. He empowered living beings to propagate 'after their kind' as plants do by producing seeds. But with the birds and fish God blessed them and said, multiply (he didn't say that to plants). These creatures would also help fill what had been a void.

In verse 22 the word 'bless' is used for the first time. God's blessing of these creatures enabled them to increase and live abundantly. He blesses us too. In the *Amplified Bible* we read that Jesus said, 'I came that they may have and enjoy life, and have it in abundance' (John 10:10) – or, as John Gowans reminds us in the chorus of his song 'We wonder why Christ came into the world' (*SASB* 274):

> He came to give us life in all its fulness,
> He came to make the blind to see,
> He came to banish death and doubt and darkness,
> He came to set his people free.
> He liberating love imparted,
> He taught men once again to smile;
> He came to bind the broken hearted,
> And God and man to reconcile.
> He came to give us life in all its fulness,
> He came to make the blind to see,
> He came to banish death and doubt and darkness,
> He came to set his people free.
> He came to set us free!

Seeds of Light

The LORD reigns, let the earth be glad;
let the distant shores rejoice.

Clouds and thick darkness surround him;
righteousness and justice are the foundation of his throne.
Fire goes before him and consumes his foes on every side.
His lightning lights up the world; the earth sees and trembles.
The mountains melt like wax before the LORD,
before the LORD of all the earth.
The heavens proclaim his righteousness,
and all the peoples see his glory.

All who worship images are put to shame,
those who boast in idols – worship him, all you gods!

Zion hears and rejoices and the villages of Judah are glad
because of your judgments, O LORD.
For you, O LORD, are the Most High over all the earth;
you are exalted far above all gods.

Let those who love the LORD hate evil,
for he guards the lives of his faithful ones
and delivers them from the hand of the wicked.
Light is shed upon the righteous
and joy on the upright in heart.
Rejoice in the LORD, you who are righteous,
and praise his holy name.

I love the word picture the *Amplified Bible* paints in verse 11: 'Light is sown for the (uncompromisingly) righteous and strewn along their pathway, and joy for the upright in heart (the irrepressible joy which comes from consciousness of His favour and protection).'

Consider how long it takes for light from the nearest stars to reach us. Then perhaps it isn't hard to imagine God sowing seeds of light in advance that will produce a harvest of light in our times of darkest need. Or can you picture him strewing light along our present pathway – enough for us to walk obediently, continuously, victoriously?

No wonder the psalmist finishes Psalm 97 with the injunction: 'Rejoice in the LORD, you consistently righteous, and give thanks at the remembrance of his holiness' (v. 12, *AB*). Amen!

All Creatures

'And God said, "Let the land produce living creatures according to their kinds: livestock, creatures that move along the ground, and wild animals, each according to its kind." And it was so' (v. 24).

Once again, God said, God made, God saw and God approved his creation. Does the image of a seal of approval come to mind? I imagine God thoroughly enjoying what he made – this time the animals. Beatrix Potter's delight with nature helped her to see things differently, and generations have been richer for her talented depiction of familiar animals and their amusing human-like antics.

Both humankind and animals were created on the final day of creation. We enjoy many characteristics in common – communication, organised societies, use of tools, home-building, travel, raising families. But humankind's intellect can be a boon or a burden to animals' survival.

Writing on 'Going Green' in the United Kingdom's *Salvationist* publication, Lieutenant-Colonel Edna Williams commented:

> God intended the earth to be inhabited. Today when many animal and plant species are driven into extinction there is serious cause for concern. Since man is the only species capable of protecting all species the implications of his compliance or neglect are enormous. Man is virtually destroying the conditions necessary for his own wellbeing . . . Only when I see and respect God in all his creation can I begin to share in his purpose for a wonderful world.

On the closest Sunday to Earth Day (referred to as Creation Sunday) some churches will take time to focus on environmental issues and affirm Christians' responsibility to preserve creation's testimony to its Creator and to declare that the God revealed in creation (Acts 17:24–27) is known fully only in the Word made flesh, in Christ the living God who made and sustains all things.

God's Word calls on all his creatures to praise him: 'Praise the LORD from the earth, you great sea creatures and all ocean depths . . . wild animals and all cattle, small creatures and flying birds' (Psalm 148:7, 10). We can enable them by helping to preserve them and their habitat through creation-care. We can value them the way God, our Maker and theirs, does.

In God's Image

*'Then God said, "Let us make man in our image, in our likeness,
and let them rule over the fish of the sea and the birds of the air,
over the livestock, over all the earth, and over all the creatures that
move along the ground"' (v. 26).*

Although the scope of the universe is mind-boggling, the focus of the biblical account of creation is on the earth, and specifically its inhabitants and God's transactions with them. When we come to God's creation of people, we gain additional insight.

The 'us' and 'our' of verse 26 refers to *Elohim* – the Divine Plurality. Up to this point in creation God's Word produced what was created, but it's different here. There's a considered united plan and purpose at work in the Godhead when producing humankind. Men and women would be God's representative managers of the earth. Our triune God created us in his image – mind and spirit.

Adam Clarke says, 'The human mind is still endowed with most extraordinary capacities; it was more so when issuing out of the hands of its Creator.'[1] And of the spirit, Milton S. Agnew says that God meant for humankind to be holy when he created us in his image. 'For he chose us in him before the creation of the world to be holy and blameless in his sight' (Ephesians 1:4). In a way, we can humbly say that God created us after his kind.

God created an astonishing body to intimately house that soul. Genesis 2's version of creation speaks of God breathing into that body the breath of life. We alone were created for deep fulfilment in union with the source of the breath of life. We pray with hymnwriter Edwin Hatch:

> Breathe on me, Breath of God,
> Fill me with life anew,
> That I may love what thou dost love,
> And do what thou wouldst do.
>
> Breathe on me, Breath of God,
> Till I am wholly thine.
> Until this earthly part of me
> Glows with thy fire divine.

Body Life

'So God created man in his own image, in the image of God he created him; male and female he created them' (v. 27).

Michelangelo's painting, *The Creation of Man*, depicts the Creator's vitalising touch awakening Adam's life. There is mystery and miracle in our bodies. In Psalm 139 David declares to the Lord: 'You created my inmost being; you knit me together in my mother's womb. I praise you because I am fearfully and wonderfully made; your works are wonderful, I know that full well' (vv. 13, 14). All our senses, organs, networks of nerves, miles of circulation and digestive tubing fit together in amazing synchronised harmony.

Our Creator means us to take our bodies seriously. But that doesn't mean indulgently, which tends to a dulling of our capacities. Paul advises, 'Therefore, I urge you, brothers, in view of God's mercy, to offer your bodies as living sacrifices, holy and pleasing to God – this is your spiritual act of worship' (Romans 12:1). The outworking of the disciplines involved in each of us becoming a 'living sacrifice' may vary from culture to culture, but the principles are similar. If we ask him, we can count on God's Spirit to help us know and do God's will.

Although we might appear different from one another in hair or skin colour, stature, bone structure or predominant facial features, we're told that nearly 99 per cent of DNA is the same across the human race. The tiny percentage of variation determines our individual features.

We are connected physically. Our life as believers should reflect our interconnections spiritually as well. We pray for one another, worship together and share each other's cares. It takes intentionality, but it could be a foretaste of heaven where we will see more of what unites than separates us as Christians.

To ponder:

What can we do to enfold those whose appearance may be different from ours into our Christian fellowship?

Husbandry

'God blessed them and said to them, "Be fruitful and increase in number; fill the earth and subdue it. Rule over the fish of the sea and the birds of the air and over every living creature that moves on the ground"' (v. 28).

Managing even a small game preserve or zoo would be daunting. But Adam and Eve, placed in Eden, were given the initial task of ruling over every living thing – fish, birds, animals. They were also the earth's first tenant gardeners – another major responsibility, since in verse 29 we learn that at this stage plants and trees were *the* source of food for human and beast.

Our first parents would have been keenly aware of their stewardship and would have concurred with Job: 'Which of all these does not know that the hand of the LORD has done this? In his hand is the life of every creature and the breath of all mankind' (Job 12:9, 10).

God's pronouncement of 'very good' over the things he'd made on this final day of creation suggests complete approval. Everything was as it was designed to be – perfect.

Humankind's right to have dominion implies an ability to do so and is an indication of something of the image of the Creator in us. It is delegated authority and humankind is accountable to God for the cultivation (not exploitation) of natural resources. God blessed the man and woman and the work he gave them to do.

Could we count all the ways God blesses us? To begin, we can wed the tune of 'Count your blessings' with Albert Orsborn's words:

> Since the Lord redeemed us from the power of sin,
> Since his Spirit sealed us other lives to win,
> Grace enough is given that we may endure,
> And we prove the promises of God are sure.
>
> All the promises of God are sure,
> Through the ages shall their truth endure;
> Hallelujah! To the heart that's pure
> All the gracious promises of God are sure.
>
> (*SASB* 755)

Further, Paul reminds us that as Christians, 'We are God's workmanship, created in Christ Jesus to do good works, which God prepared in advance for us to do' (Ephesians 2:10).

Gift of Sabbath

'And God blessed the seventh day and made it holy, because on it he rested from all the work of creating that he had done' (v. 3).

The first three verses of Genesis 2 could be viewed as the conclusion of Genesis 1. God ended his work and rested on the seventh day. Can we say that God's final act of creation was the separation of a day of rest? Six days are given to humankind for oversight of what God created, but the seventh day is for reflecting on our relationship with the Creator himself.

Our key verse tells us that God blessed the seventh day. Yes, on previous days God blessed what he made and called what he had created 'very good' but he made only the seventh day 'holy'.

In Exodus 16 the Israelites in the wilderness are told to gather extra manna, enough for the next day, because the seventh day was a day of solemn rest, a holy day of worship dedicated to the Lord. In Exodus 20 the reasons given for observing Sabbath are that God directed it and observed it himself at creation. In Exodus 31 we are told Sabbath-keeping is a sign that the Lord sets his people apart. In Deuteronomy 5 the reason given is that God's people are to remember that he delivered them from bondage in Egypt where they never had time off. We sense that Sabbath-keeping holds multiple benefits.

The seventh day deals with time rather than space. The rhythm of night and day is important to our well-being. We function best when rest and work are given proper portions of our day. The body rested and restored assists the Spirit's work. The rhythm of weeks needs to be regular too. Other important days of the year fluctuate with the seasons, but one day in seven is established as significant and separate.

For the Church, the basis of Sabbath-keeping has changed from celebrating creation to celebrating Christ's resurrection. The principle of managing what God has made for six days and celebrating God himself on the seventh remains. It is still to be a day of joy, renewal, praise. Is it time to evaluate the way we view and use God's gift?

Hand-crafted

'The LORD God formed the man from the dust of the ground and breathed into his nostrils the breath of life, and the man became a living being' (v. 7).

The description of creation in Genesis 2 parallels some parts of Genesis 1, but in this chapter the focus is on man, the pinnacle of creation, and his relationship with the Creator. When you read, 'The LORD formed the man', does that make you think of a potter or sculptor shaping pliable clay? People as clay in God's hands is a choice biblical metaphor: 'Yet, O LORD, you are our Father. We are the clay, you are the potter; we are all the work of your hand' (Isaiah 64:8).

'Adam' (a term used both for the first man and for humankind) comes from *adamah* meaning earth and implying a ruddy colour. Raw clay has little value, but it can be made into objects of great value. The potter or sculptor gives it value.

Occasionally a potter breathes onto the clay turning on the wheel. The pressure of the warm air expands the form lightly and makes the piece seem to come alive. Other potters seal the form to trap their breath within it giving resilience to the shape and allowing it to be worked up into a taller form without collapsing. Later a new opening is made.

God formed man from the dust of the ground. Humans and animals have some basic chemical elements in common with soil; but the distinguishing feature of humans is their living souls. Other creatures have breath but only humans are God-breathed physical and spiritual beings with capacity for eternal life.

In 1 Corinthians 15:45–49 Paul explains that Adam represents all humanity as a mortal being made from, and returning to, dust. On the other hand, the risen Christ (the second Adam) will give everyone who believes in him an eternal body fit for heaven.

All that I am, all I can be,
All that I have, all that is me,
Accept and use, Lord,
As you would choose, Lord, right now today!
Take every passion, every skill,
Take all my dreams and bend them to your will.
My all I give, Lord, for you I'll live, Lord,
Come what may.

William Himes

A Psalm of David

A Salvation Army officer in Tokyo gave a poignant testimony about his experience as a cadet. Wondering about his calling to ministry, he had gone to the roof of a building to think and look into the night sky. He was overwhelmed with a sense of God's majesty and greatness and his own comparatively infinitesimal life.

Psalm 8 came alive and spoke to his heart as he marvelled that, through Christ, he had been included in God's amazing plan. That assurance enabled him to continue humbly and effectively to serve the Lord and the people.

> O LORD, our LORD,
> how majestic is your name in all the earth!
>
> You have set your glory above the heavens.
> From the lips of children and infants
> you have ordained praise
> because of your enemies,
> to silence the foe and the avenger.
>
> When I consider your heavens,
> the work of your fingers,
> the moon and the stars, which you have set in place,
> what is man that you are mindful of him,
> the son of man that you care for him?
> You made him a little lower than the heavenly beings
> and crowned him with glory and honour.
>
> You made him ruler over the works of your hands;
> you put everything under his feet:
> all flocks and herds, and the beasts of the field,
> the birds of the air, and the fish of the sea,
> all that swim the paths of the seas.
>
> O LORD, our LORD,
> how majestic is your name in all the earth!

Paradise

'Now the LORD God had planted a garden in the east, in Eden; and there he put the man he had formed' (v. 8).

In verse 8, the word sometimes translated as garden is from a Persian word for paradise and connotes an enclosed garden or park. Jesus told the repentant thief on the cross that he would be with him in paradise (Luke 23:39–43). Was the garden a type of heaven? Was it perfect in what it contained as well as what it didn't? We may imagine the fertile acres as free from disease and disaster, poisonous plants and animals, choking weeds and vines. Several Old Testament prophets (Isaiah, Ezekiel, Joel) allude to its perfect state.

Where was this original planned ideal space? It was in a region known as Eden. Some people think this could have been in Mesopotamia (present-day Iraq). Others suggest it was in Armenia (present-day Turkey and Armenia). The rivers noted in this chapter come from the rugged mountainous region there – the same general region of Ararat, where Noah's ark came to rest. Wherever the region was located, a river flowed from there to water the garden, then outside the garden it divided into four rivers.

Does the scene remind us of Ezekiel's vision of water flowing from the temple (Ezekiel 47) or of John's picture of a pure river of water of life flowing from under the throne of God (Revelation 22)?

In the middle of the garden of delight where God made all kinds of trees grow were two especially significant trees – the tree of life and the tree of the knowledge of good and evil. The tree of life, or life-giving tree, also described in Ezekiel's vision and John's revelation, is mentioned several times in Proverbs where it represents a source of hope and help. In the garden it was a sign of the eternal life men and women can have if obedient to the Creator. It may have originally been meant for a source of health, a fountain of youth.

My Christ, he is the tree of life,
Which in God's garden grows,
Whose fruits do feed, whose leaves do heal,
My Christ is Sharon's rose.

John Mason

Perfect Names

'So the man gave names to all the livestock, the birds of the air and all the beasts of the field. But for Adam no suitable helper was found' (v. 20).

Yesterday we thought about the tree of life. The other significant tree in the garden was the tree of knowledge of good and evil. Even its name encompasses extreme opposites and so symbolises completeness and omniscience. It was this tree's fruit that God clearly forbade man to eat, on penalty of death.

God's warning about the prohibited tree came between two tasks he gave Adam. The responsibilities highlighted something of the image of God in him: the tasks of cultivating the garden and naming the animals. God credited Adam's discernment of the nature of each animal and choice of a suitable name (in Hebrew, as in other languages, the name and character or characteristics coincided).

How long did the process take? Did Adam enjoy toying with names? Was it exhausting work? Afterwards it was noted that no suitable helper was found for man and that God caused him to fall into a deep sleep. God made woman from one of Adam's ribs.

When presented with his complementary human being, Adam said she would be called woman because she was taken out of his flesh and bone. We don't know if his naming her 'woman' (in English, possible contraction of womb-man) implied discernment or something else. However, we do infer Adam's clear-cut approval of his partner. No wedding day disaster here!

In the next chapter of Genesis, after their sin and sentence, Adam gives woman a specific name. Not a name taken from nature or indicating her character. He calls her Eve, meaning life or mother of all living. Were there intimations of hope that humanity would continue? Unwittingly, did her name imply that through her descendants the hope of life would come? 'Jesus answered, "I am the way and the truth and the life. No one comes to the Father except through me"' (John 14:6).

Deceived

'Then the Lord God said to the woman, "What is this you have done?"
The woman said, "The serpent deceived me, and I ate"' (v. 13).

Much of creation continues and grows automatically, but people grow by decisions. Although we have divinely implanted instincts and genes and are as subject to natural laws as the rest of creation, humans are unique in that only we are given the ability to freely choose.

Obviously Eve was given free will. Although Scripture does not record that Eve received God's prohibition directly, which may have made her easier prey for Satan, we can tell from her replies to Satan that she was certainly aware of God's command. Would she have fared better if she hadn't been alone? It's doubtful that Adam would have prevented the sin, for when he arrived he assented to it and participated too.

The source of temptation is shown to be distinct from God and his creation. Satan introduced an alternative to God's way. Eve was deceived, some say framed. But however cunning the 'angel of light' was, Eve chose to believe his lies and put her will above God's. Satan initiated the conversation subtly and stirred resentment against God's restraints. He implied that there was more to be experienced than they had thus far. Also, that they wouldn't lose their current joys but add to them as the gods they deserved to be. At this, disobedience and desire overrode discernment.

Eve heard the alternative message, mulled it over with some intellectual curiosity and cunning, visualised taking the fruit, and, convinced, rationalised its worth to her, asserted herself to possess it, then ate it and shared it. Do we recognise the pattern?

Although falling prey to evil may have been gradual, Adam and Eve quickly discovered when they sinned that believing Satan's lies had opened their eyes but confused their minds. Now they knew guilt, fear and shame. They should have run to their Maker, but they didn't, they hid. Yet God reached out to them, as he still does in grace to us. Praise him!

Relieved

*'The LORD God made garments of skin for Adam and his wife
and clothed them' (v. 21).*

How long did Satan's deception of Eve take? Did he plan to wear her down gradually? Had he become a familiar part of the scene? Was Adam unaware, unconcerned or preoccupied? When God confronted the first couple they admitted shame, but didn't own the blame. Did humankind regret the sin or just the consequences at first?

Adam and Eve almost seemed relieved to be found out and even to be punished. Because of who God is, everyone involved received appropriate judgment. A holy God dealt with sin justly. God cursed the serpent and alluded to his future complete demise. Evil would not have the final victory. Jesus came to destroy the devil's work.

Woman's sentence involved pain in childbirth and a dependence on man – perhaps a rebuke to her aggressive wrong choices. The ground was cursed because of man who had listened to his wife and acquiesced to sin. Man's sentence involved the frustration of work thwarted by thorns and thistles. Providing for his family would be hard work all his life. God also announced that man's body would return to the ground. Although spiritual death, separation from God, was immediate, physical death would be eventual but as certain.

In acts of grace and mercy, God made Adam and Eve animal skin coverings for protection and banished them from the paradise of Eden. He set guards – angels and a flaming sword – so they wouldn't be able to eat from the tree of life and live forever in their fallen state.

Jesus Christ has overturned Satan's deception and gives those who trust him as Saviour the promise of access to the tree of life. God's intent for humankind to live in beauty and peace would yet be accomplished. As Christians, led by the Holy Spirit, we can know a foretaste of his kingdom now (1 John 3).

Brothers

'Later she gave birth to his brother Abel. Now Abel kept flocks,
and Cain worked the soil' (v. 2).

The world's first baby was Cain (meaning 'acquisition'). Eve said she acquired him with the help of the Lord. Their second child was Abel (meaning 'vapour'). Some think the boys were twins. Their very different temperaments remind us of another set of famous twins – Jacob and Esau.

In the garden, Adam had been charged with oversight of animals and plants. Now one son worked with plants and the other with animals. No doubt their parents attempted to describe the paradise they had lost and the importance of acknowledging the Lord and his material and spiritual provisions.

In the process of time (v. 3), on the day of offering the boys brought offerings to worship the Lord. The word for offering (*minchah*) was similar to the one used later in Leviticus to describe the thank offering. The offering could have been given in recognition of the Creator's gifts. Some commentators believe Abel brought his *minchah* and an additional offering from his flock. The animal offering could have implied need for divine mercy. In Hebrews 11:4 the writer tells of God commending Abel as righteous and speaking well of his offerings (plural).

God, aware of motives, didn't accept Cain's offering. This angered Cain, but God offered counsel and gave him a chance for change. If there had been sibling rivalry before, Cain, unwilling to take second place to anyone – especially his younger brother – displayed rage and arrogance over humble Abel's better standing with God.

That Cain knew murder was wrong is evidenced by his choice of an isolated location for the crime and the fact that he hid Abel's body. Judgment followed. What irony that the tiller of soil buried his brother in the loam! Part of his punishment involved no longer being successful at cultivating the ground. He would be haunted by the unbearable memory of his crime and would be away from his family and God's presence.

Cain was full of fear and self-pity. In mercy, God tempered Cain's punishment with his token to assure his physical safety.

Music to our Hearts

*'His brother's name was Jubal; he was the father of all who
play the harp and flute' (v. 21).*

Cain went east to what the Bible translator Moffatt calls wanderland. He started
a family that six generations later included a daughter (Naamah) and her
three noteworthy brothers. One (Jabal) was known as the father of those who live
in tents, have cattle and purchase possessions. Another (Jubal) was known as the
father of all who play stringed and woodwind instruments. And the third (*Tubal-
cain*) was the forger of bronze and iron tools. What a family!

Since these things are mentioned, they must have been noteworthy, or at least
quite different from what the norm had been to that point. We grasp the basic
practicality of developing convenient dwellings, of raising animals for food and
profit, and of working out systems of barter or currency to obtain necessities.
Making sturdy implements to aid their existence makes sense as well. But would
we have imagined music to be one of the initial gifts humankind developed?

Did the earliest music imitate pleasing sounds in nature? Did it aid recall when
telling stories? It's difficult for us today to imagine a time when music wasn't
prevalent. Music delights us, inspires us and moves us to tears. It enters under the
radar and heads through our senses to our emotions. We know music can cross
barriers of language, culture, ages.

Maybe it transcends mere perception because it connects with our neuro-
biology. Some people enjoy music with more than one of their five senses –
identifying musical intervals by the flavours they produce on the tongue or seeing
individual notes as colours. In a novel set in the time of the patriarchs, a character
who heard harmony for the first time described the beauty of hearing such singing
as a piece of fabric woven with all the colours of a rainbow.

Thank God for the gift of music in its multifaceted forms, and especially for
musicians who use their abilities to glorify him. Whether we are music-makers or
appreciative listeners, can we take time this week to intentionally absorb excellent
music and value its source? Then in worship, 'Sing and make music in your heart
to the Lord' (Ephesians 5:19).

O Sifuni Mungu

O Sifuni Mungu is an exuberant, syncopated vocal work. In the arrangement, Francis of Assisi's 'All creatures of our God and King' is paired with an African (Swahili) chorus and the combination changes the metre and tempo for an exciting rendition nearly five minutes in duration. Think of an awakened creation singing:

> All creatures of our God and King,
> Lift up your voice and with us sing
> Alleluia, alleluia!
> Thou burning sun with golden beam,
> Thou silver moon with softer gleam:
>
> O praise him, O praise him,
> Alleluia, alleluia, alleluia!
>
> Thou rushing wind that art so strong,
> Ye clouds that sail in heaven along,
> O praise him, alleluia!
> Thou rising morn, in praise rejoice,
> Ye lights of evening, find a voice:
>
> Thou flowing water, pure and clear,
> Make music for thy Lord to hear,
> Alleluia, alleluia!
> Thou fire so masterful and bright,
> That givest man both warmth and light:
>
> Dear mother earth, who day by day
> Unfoldest blessings on our way,
> O praise him, alleluia!
> The flowers and fruits that in thee grow,
> Let them his glory also show.
>
> Let all things their Creator bless,
> And worship him in humbleness,
> O praise him, alleluia!
> Praise, praise the Father, praise the Son,
> And praise the Spirit, Three in One.

Next in Line

'When Adam had lived 130 years, he had a son in his own likeness,
in his own image; and he named him Seth' (5:3).

In Genesis 4:25 Eve says their son whom Adam named Seth (meaning 'placed' or 'appointed') replaced Abel. Seth became more than a replacement for a lost child. His line would eventually include godly Enoch and Noah. Only Seth's descendants would continue after the flood. Looking back we know the Messiah came through Seth. Eve couldn't have known any of that, could she?

New Testament family trees note the offspring through whom Jesus Christ, the Child of Promise, came. Included, for example, are Shem, Noah's middle son; Jacob, second of Isaac's twin boys; Judah, Jacob's fourth son; and David, Jesse's eighth. In many cultures the eldest child holds a special place in the family – a place of inherent privilege and responsibility. That seems to have been a tradition in biblical families as well, but not always.

Although birth order placement in a family may affect temperament and achievement, it doesn't determine it. Apparently the firstborn weren't singled out as the only ones to be in the Messiah's line. It was more about God's grace than inherent rights.

Were you longed for, adopted, a surprise, a miracle, one of many or the only one? In a remarkable way Jesus is uniquely fit to understand all these positions.

Jesus said, 'Whoever does God's will is my brother and sister and mother' (Mark 3:35). The initial step of doing God's will and entering God's family hinges on our repentance of sin, and faith in Christ as our Saviour. 'Yet to all who received him, to those who believed in his name, he gave the right to become children of God – children born not of natural descent, nor of human decision or a husband's will, but born of God' (John 1:12, 13).

Do you notice a family resemblance in his obedient followers? 'For those God foreknew he also predestined to be conformed to the likeness of his Son, that he might be the firstborn among many brothers' (Romans 8:29).

Growing like him who my pattern shall be,
Till in his beauty my King I shall see!
Eliza Edmunds Hewitt

Young and Old

'Enoch walked with God; then he was no more, because
God took him away' (v. 24).

There are many theories about the longevity of those named in the selective genealogies of this chapter. Whatever the explanation, we note that in spite of significant length of life there was seemingly minimal faith. Of those mentioned, Methuselah's life was the longest (969 years) and Enoch's the briefest (365 years). Despite having the shortest life, Enoch has the most glowing witness – he walked with God.

Verse 22 indicates that Enoch's 300-year walk with God began or became his default mode at age sixty-five after his son Methuselah was born. We wonder if having his first child had anything to do with Enoch's new way of life. The miracle of birth makes many hearts tender.

What does walking with God mean? It means exercising faith in him and his purposes. It means spending time with him and delighting in his companionship. It means going places with God. As William Booth said to his daughter Evangeline, 'Progress is made by keeping pace with the stride of God.' It means having a testimony of God's supremacy (Isaiah 52:7).

We have the added privilege of the written Word as basic to our walk with God. But even without the written revealed Word, Enoch read God's book of creation. Did Enoch pay attention to what God made? Did he listen appreciatively to the sounds of children's laughter, to wind in the trees? Did he relish the scent of ripe fruit, of pine needles underfoot? Did he stop to touch a rock, the bark of a tree? Did he savour fresh bread or cool water? Do we?

Enoch had no gravesite, but his epitaph is a lasting witness – Enoch, whose name means 'dedicated', walked with God, and as Hebrews 11:5 adds, 'before he was taken, he was commended as one who pleased God'.

To ponder:

Beside thee as I walk,
I will delight in thee.

Albert Orsborn (SASB 59)

Tidings of Comfort and Rest

'He named him Noah and said, "He will comfort us in the labour and painful toil of our hands caused by the ground the LORD has cursed"' (v. 29).

Methuselah's name meant 'death is sent', yet he lived for 969 years. Since the flood came the year he died, his name's significance may have related to that. His grandson Noah lived almost as long as Methuselah – 950 years. And Noah shared an enviable family likeness with his grandfather's father, Enoch, who walked with God. That was said of Noah as well (Genesis 6:9).

Noah's name (meaning 'comfort' or 'bringer of rest'), seems to forecast a mission of hope or respite in the middle of tragedy. Someone suggested that comfort means sighing with someone. Perhaps that is true during times of stress or suffering. Can we picture Noah sighing with his family or with the animals during preparations for riding out the flood? Perhaps, since life would not be as they'd known it.

Yet our word 'comfort' comes from the Latin word meaning 'with strength'. Musicians might think of *forte* dynamic markings that direct them to play more forcefully. Bible commentator William Barclay reminds us that true Christian comfort is no easy and sentimental thing but something which puts courage into a person when life is threatening to take courage away. So our worship should include that type of durable comfort.

Today, read – or maybe sing? – two verses of Martin Luther's 'A mighty fortress is our God' and be strengthened (comforted) by Christ Jesus, 'that Word', whose kingdom is forever:

A mighty fortress is our God,
A bulwark never failing;
Our helper he, amid the flood
Of mortal ills prevailing.
For still our ancient foe
Doth seek to work us woe;
His craft and power are great,
And armed with cruel hate,
On earth is not his equal.

That word above all earthly powers,
No thanks to them abideth;
The Spirit and the gifts are ours
Through him who with us sideth.
Let goods and kindred go,
This mortal life also;
The body they may kill;
God's truth abideth still,
His kingdom is forever.

Divine Design

'By faith Noah, when warned about things not yet seen, in holy fear built an ark to save his family. By his faith he condemned the world and became heir of the righteousness that comes by faith' (Hebrews 11:7).

The story of Noah's ark, which we've known since childhood, might evoke children's television-like images of a tidy floating zoo, as if the focus was animals on a cruise. However, although God cares for all his creatures, Scripture indicates that the chief issues precipitating the flood regarded humankind. God saw that every inclination of human thoughts was evil, and regretted making humankind at all. God saw the rampant violence and widespread corruption in the world. If the description reminds us of current world news, what is the Christian's response?

The situation in Noah's day grieved God and gave him pain. People seemed oblivious to their condition. Jesus tells us that a similar time will come again:

As it was in the days of Noah, so it will be at the coming of the Son of Man. For in the days before the flood, people were eating and drinking, marrying and giving in marriage, up to the day Noah entered the ark; and they knew nothing about what would happen until the flood came and took them all away. That is how it will be at the coming of the Son of Man. (Matthew 24:37–39)

Noah was a righteous man, blameless among the people of his time. He walked with God. God could communicate with him. When God initiated the conversation about destroying the earth, he didn't just share with him a plan of judgment and destruction, but one of deliverance.

God was not obliged to share his strategy, but did, and involved Noah in preparing the way of rescue. God gave specific instructions about such things as the type of wood to be used, dimensions, number of decks, waterproofing, and where the door and window would be placed. Since this was an original, Noah could not have had a mental picture for the ark. His participation required his faith, obedience and diligence.

God has given today's believers opportunity to participate in rescue as well. Besides our most important task of sharing the good news of Christ, there are many practical ways of entering into the issues facing others. Ask him.

The Coming Storm

' "*Seven days from now I will send rain on the earth for forty days
and forty nights, and I will wipe from the face of the earth every
living creature I have made*" ' (v. 4).

Noah's tools could be set aside. The one-of-a-kind structure he had built was finished. It was time to settle in. How did the animals know to come to the ark? Did they have a sense of an approaching calamity, such as some have just before a tsunami strikes, causing them to head for higher ground? God had brought the animals to Adam to be named; did he bring them to the ark to be saved? Did Noah receive special instructions about the food each would need? Feeding household pets or even birds that winter in our gardens is enough of a job. Did the creatures sleep through the storm? We wonder about such details.

Perhaps it was the Sabbath and they were worshipping and resting when God told 600-year-old Noah that the long-expected event was just a week away. Since rain wasn't mentioned before, we don't know if they understood what it meant or what forty days of it would do, but at least they were given a sense of its duration. Sometimes knowing difficult times aren't interminable helps us cope. No doubt it was a very busy week. Once the eight family members, scores of animals and provisions were assembled, they had seven days to embark before the coming cataclysm.

Has the Lord given you a word about a coming challenge? Does it seem too great or have too many unknowns? In *Experiencing God*, Henry Blackaby writes:

If the assignment I sense God is giving me is something I know I can handle, I know it probably is not from God. The kind of assignments God gives in the Bible are always God-sized. They are beyond what people can do because he wants to demonstrate his nature, his strength, his provision, his kindness to his people and to a watching world. That is the only way the world will come to know him.[2]

Amen!

Begone, unbelief, my Saviour is near,
And for my relief will surely appear;
By prayer let me wrestle, And he will perform;
With Christ in the vessel, I smile at the storm.
John Newton

Wages of Life

*'For forty days the flood kept coming on the earth, and as the waters
increased they lifted the ark high above the earth' (v. 17).*

There had been enough anticipation, enough preparation. They entered the ark
and God closed them in. The rain came, just as God had forecast. It must have
been a day of wonder, especially if it was humankind's first experience with rain.
Did Noah's family notice things around them behaving differently just before the
rain – leaves turning over, wind shifting, clouds mounting, a new strange smell in
the air?

Before man was created, on days two and three of creation, God divided the
waters above from the waters below then collected the waters on earth, separating
them from the land. Now the waters seem to have reverted to the primal state as
the fountains of the deep opened and joined the water from above.

The ark on dry land might have seemed odd accommodation but as the waters
lifted it, a floating barn without propulsion, it was the only safe place left on earth.
Only God could have known.

Peter called Noah a preacher of righteousness (2 Peter 2:5), so we assume he
relayed God's message about the coming judgment, even without apparent
converts. Noah obeyed God. His reward was life. It is ours as well.

Noah could have joined us in the timeless words of Stanley E. Ditmer's song:

> I shall not fear though darkened clouds may gather round me;
> The God I serve is one who cares and understands.
> Although the storms I face would threaten to confound me,
> Of this I am assured: I'm in his hands.
>
> I'm in his hands, I'm in his hands;
> Whate'er the future holds
> I'm in his hands,
> The days I cannot see
> Have all been planned for me;
> His way is best, you see;
> I'm in his hands.

> (*SASB* 732)

Witness of Works and Word

The heavens declare the glory of God;
the skies proclaim the work of his hands.
Day after day they pour forth speech;
night after night they display knowledge.
There is no speech or language where their voice is not heard.
Their voice goes out into all the earth,
their words to the ends of the world.

In the heavens he has pitched a tent for the sun,
which is like a bridegroom coming forth from his pavilion,
like a champion rejoicing to run his course.
It rises at one end of the heavens
and makes its circuit to the other; nothing is hidden from its heat.

The law of the LORD is perfect, reviving the soul.
The statutes of the LORD are trustworthy, making wise the simple.
The precepts of the LORD are right, giving joy to the heart.
The commands of the LORD are radiant, giving light to the eyes.
The fear of the LORD is pure, enduring for ever.
The ordinances of the LORD are sure and altogether righteous.
They are more precious than gold, than much pure gold;
they are sweeter than honey, than honey from the comb.
By them is your servant warned;
in keeping them there is great reward.

Who can discern his errors?
Forgive my hidden faults.
Keep your servant also from wilful sins;
may they not rule over me.
Then will I be blameless, innocent of great transgression.

May the words of my mouth and the meditation of my heart
be pleasing in your sight,
O LORD, my Rock and my Redeemer.

Blessed Thud

*'And on the seventeenth day of the seventh month the ark
came to rest on the mountains of Ararat' (v. 4).*

Forty days of rain stopped. God remembered Noah and sent a drying wind. Although it took much longer to dry the earth than it had to flood it, God's followers were not forgotten or outside his providential care. Neither are we.

Have you ever taken a long flight and known the relief of touching down, even if the landing gear bounced a bit along the runway? Noah and his family had been on board for 150 days before the waters receded enough for the ark to rest on mountains. What a blessed jolt of relief when the ark stopped on Ararat – a mountainous area of Armenia! Seasickness would end. They wouldn't be like albatrosses permanently living on the ocean. The women on board would tend the earth again, plant seeds and watch them grow.

Their next thoughts were surely of disembarking, but it would be more than two months before they could see the mountain tops, and much longer before they could stand on land. But they had felt the blessed jolt!

Some situations (usually the unpleasant or difficult ones) seem interminable, but God gives us tokens of his care along the way to reassure us. Often it's through Scripture, which comes alive for us in our particular need. Sometimes God uses strangers. Have you received unsolicited kindness from someone you might never meet again? Has the Lord encouraged your heart through music? Has he used unexpected shafts of sunlight streaming through clouds, or an email from a friend? Has the fragrance of something unseen along the path made you smile and prompted you to think of God's goodness? James reminds us, 'Every good and perfect gift is from above, coming down from the Father of the heavenly lights, who does not change like shifting shadows' (1:17).

Do you need assurance of God's presence and power today? Prayerfully read his Word and stay alert to the innumerable gifts he sends as tokens of his care. They may even come as blessed thuds.

Open the Window

'After forty days Noah opened the window he had made in the ark' (v. 6).

They had waited forty days for the rain to stop. Then, without sail or rudder, they'd floated for months until the ark stopped on the mountains. A couple more months' wait followed, when perhaps they took turns looking out through the ventilation space under the roof, until the waters receded enough for them to see the tops of the mountains poking out of the water.

And still Noah waited forty more days before testing his hypothesis. Perhaps his family found Noah's discipline of delay as difficult to cope with as we would (it's a test of our patience just to remain seated in a plane that's landed until the captain turns out the 'fasten seatbelt' light).

But delay is not denial. We have no indication that God told Noah to wait, but neither had he said, 'Go out.' Noah had known God's instruction before. He walked with God and didn't need to run ahead, but could trust him to give direction at the right time. Meanwhile he used what he had, and did what he could.

Noah opened the window and dispatched a raven, an intelligent carrion eater who found enough to eat without the ark's fare and didn't return. Then Noah sent out the seed-eating dove, and it returned immediately. A week later he tried again. This time the dove didn't return until evening and brought back a fresh olive leaf. Did the family pass around this recognisable green leaf and talk about its significance?

The ground was drying. Perhaps some things would be as they had remembered them, or even better. When he sent the dove out again and it didn't return, Noah lifted the covering of the ark. The earth was dry. Soon he would hear from the Lord.

Waiting for deliverance or for direction? Open the window at hand. Use what you already know. Trust God to provide what you'll need next.

Carved into the beam of a hillside summer chapel by the sea in northern Japan I noticed an English paraphrase of the Japanese version of Proverbs 4:12: 'As thou goest, step by step, I will open up thy way before thee.' Amen.

Second Chances

'"Bring out every kind of living creature that is with you – the birds, the animals, and all the creatures that move along the ground – so they can multiply on the earth and be fruitful and increase in number upon it"' (v. 17).

Finally, after more than 365 days in the ark, the long-anticipated word came. God had not only remembered them and sent the wind to dry the earth, but now said go out and bring out. Did the creatures feel at home when they left the ark on Ararat? After all, Eden may have been in that very region. Nishan Der Garabedian – the early-day Salvation Army fez-sporting evangelist, Armenian-born 'Joe the Turk' – would have loved the idea that Eden and then Ararat were in his homeland!

Did the animals hesitate? They followed Noah's lead and went out by families (v. 19, *NKJV*) so it seems they disembarked in an orderly way. Did they step on terra firma gingerly, or prance with wild abandon? Imagine the fresh world through the eyes of released wild animals.

We don't know what Noah expected to find after the flood. Would it be a new world or a restored one? If God created the earth, couldn't he just recreate it? In a way he did and does and will. Noah may have shared a measure of Adam's sense of wonder and newness even though he was past the age of 600. The mandate God had given animals in Eden to be fruitful and multiply was repeated to those released from the ark. Earth wasn't back to its original sinless state. It would still be dysfunctional. But God had not given up on humankind.

When writer Philip Yancey read Genesis in natural environs for the first time, he realised that God's gift of choice to humankind caused him to have to repair the damage of sin at great personal cost and that although God has a plan of restoration, it's a long way between Genesis creation and Revelation recreation.

What spiritual lessons had Noah and family learned after a year afloat? God is trustworthy. God's plans succeed. God is able to do the impossible. God enables second chances. What have we learned in our recent challenges?

First Act, First Vow

' *"As long as the earth endures, seedtime and harvest, cold and heat,*
summer and winter, day and night will never cease" ' *(v. 22).*

Noah and company had been incommunicado with the vanished world outside the ark. They were even more cut off than early missionaries who had no telephones, airmail or email – just a rare letter transported by sea. Noah's family had no one to communicate with except God. Had they missed the Sabbath worship while afloat? Noah's first act after arriving on dry land was to build an altar and offer sacrifice.

In Jewish tradition, the place where Noah built his altar was the same place where Adam built the one his family used. Perhaps the rocks they used were similar. Where would Noah find fuel, with everything recently waterlogged? It's logical that he used wood from the ark.

With the limited stock of animals for the great task of repopulating the earth, we still find Noah choosing some of every family of clean birds and animals for sacrifice. He gave evidence of carefulness and generosity in his worship.

God always notices when people worship him from their hearts. Jesus watched how the crowd, especially the wealthy, gave offerings ostentatiously at the temple in Jerusalem. But his commendation was for a poverty-stricken widow who placed her tiny coins in the treasury. He said she had given the most that day because she had given all (Mark 12:41–44).

> If on our daily course our mind
> Be set to hallow all we find,
> New treasures still of countless price
> God will provide for sacrifice.
> *John Keble*

Noah's sacrifice communicated a sweet fragrance to God. This is the same term used of the sacrifice of Christ in Ephesians 5:2. God was pleased with it and vowed to himself never to curse the ground, never to bring another worldwide flood and, while earth lasts, never to interrupt the rhythm of seasons and days. This must have especially reassured Noah and family since they had missed a full year of earth's life cycle.

Cherished

*' "And from each man, too, I will demand an accounting for the
life of his fellow man" ' (v. 5).*

God told Noah to release the animals so they could abound. He knew they
would multiply naturally. God also gave Noah's family a dictate to be fruitful
and multiply (he had given the same word to Adam in Genesis 1:28). Did God
think they would be afraid to raise families after the flood? Did the eight survivors
comprehend their tenuous position as progenitors of the human race? For
emphasis, God gave the command twice (vv. 1, 7).

God also said that from now on animals would fear humankind. He followed
that with a corollary – people could now eat meat. They would go from being
gamekeepers to hunters (not for sport, but food) once there were plenty of
animals.

At the outset of our biosphere it seems humans and animals were vegetarians.
God gave Adam all seed-bearing plants and fruit trees as food (Genesis 1:29). We
don't know if that changed for the animals after the fall, but God waited until now
to add meat to the human diet. Was the vegetation after the flood less nutritious
or plentiful? Would humankind's activities now require more protein? We can
only conjecture.

But even with this expanded permission, people were not to eat the blood of
animals. Restrictions about eating only clean animals were still many generations
away. The description of some of the animals entering the ark as clean would have
referred to those acceptable for sacrifice (Genesis 8:20).

God put the fear of humans into animals. Then, so men and women wouldn't
destroy each other, he put the fear of God into them, with warnings against
brutality and arbitrary killing. Such violence had been rampant before the flood
and God deplored it. Murder had existed even in the first family. Taking the life of
anyone made in his image would be judged. God would share the judgment for
murder with humankind and allow the human community to execute earthly
justice.

We're meant to treasure life as a gift from God. Each person's life is to be
cherished, nurtured and redeemed. What does this say to our age's predisposition
to abortion, euthanasia or human trafficking? How can we better display Christ's
love to those whom society discards?

Rainbows

'So God said to Noah, "This is the sign of the covenant I have established between me and all life on the earth"' (v. 17).

Not only did the family of Noah see other mountaintops from Ararat, but after worshipping God at the top of the world they saw the first rainbow. Would the bow be most complete and striking from a mountain top? They would face valley days and stormy ones, but they had seen the vista and the bow of promise from the summit. They would always know that with God there is more to life than the present moment.

One snowy March afternoon a ball struck our eight-year-old son in the eye. Later he complained that the letters on a menu were blurry. He had lost vision in that eye. One doctor led to another. The specialist said it was non-correctable and ordered a brain scan. My husband and I, and loved ones far away, prayed for restoration and proceeded with the disconcerting tests. Work, school, family life went on. Rain prevailed over sun when we came out of the paediatrician's office without answers or direction.

Chiefly the Holy Spirit strengthens me as I read the Word. Occasionally the Lord uses music, poetry, nature or his Church to encourage my faith. Uncharacteristically and on impulse I asked the Lord to let us see a rainbow if in the end, whatever it entailed, everything would be all right. We saw one as we drove home. I felt great peace about the eventual outcome, however long it might take.

The tests for tumours were negative. What could we do next? We visited the ophthalmologist for a repeat examination. Our son's vision returned without apparent reason. We told the doctor we had prayed, and he said that could not have hurt. An understatement! Twenty-five years later our son's eyesight remains fine. A verse of George Matheson's hymn has been poignant for us ever since:

> O Joy that seekest me through pain,
> I cannot close my heart to thee;
> I trace the rainbow through the rain
> And feel the promise is not vain,
> That morn shall tearless be.

Whose Robe is the Light

Psalm 104:1–5 formed the basis of Robert Grant's hymn, 'O worship the King'. It is a commentary on creation and a metrical version of the psalm.

> O worship the King, all glorious above;
> O gratefully sing his power and his love;
> Our shield and defender, the Ancient of Days,
> Pavilioned in splendour and girded with praise.
>
> O tell of his might, O sing of his grace,
> Whose robe is the light, whose canopy space;
> His chariots of wrath the deep thunderclouds form,
> And dark is his path on the wings of the storm.
>
> The earth with its store of wonders untold,
> Almighty, thy power hath founded of old,
> Hath stablished it fast by a changeless decree,
> And round it hath cast, like a mantle, the sea.
>
> Thy bountiful care what tongue can recite?
> It breathes in the air, it shines in the light,
> It streams from the hills, it descends to the plain,
> And sweetly distils in the dew and the rain.
>
> Frail children of dust and feeble as frail,
> In thee do we trust, nor find thee to fail;
> Thy mercies how tender, how firm to the end,
> Our Maker, Defender, Redeemer and Friend.
>
> O measureless Might! Ineffable Love!
> While angels delight to hymn thee above,
> The humbler creation, though feeble their lays,
> With true adoration shall sing to thy praise.

Viticulture

'Noah, a man of the soil, proceeded to plant a vineyard' (v. 20).

It takes time to grow a vineyard. It's a year-round job requiring intentional care. Soil on stony hillsides where erosion has worn down the land is suitable for flourishing vineyards. A vine struggling to grow there produces brighter-coloured grapes with better-flavoured juice than one grown in richer soil. Noah would have readily found appropriate conditions.

He may have had some knowledge of grape-growing before his ark-construction days. If so, he would have known to nip off the buds from the vines for the first two years to force the vine's vigour into root and leaf production. Noah knew the perpetual seasons God had promised would continue (Genesis 8:22), so perhaps a man over 600 years old could be patient.

Vines don't seek to be pruned and pruning isn't easy for the vinedresser. To train the young and maintain the mature, the viticulturalist must know the vines and not let them send runners in every direction but keep them centred on their task. Wild grape vines, which aren't pruned, send out tendrils wherever they can. They entwine tree limbs and, although they may provide material for decorations, they don't produce useful fruit.

We humans would rather not be pruned or restricted, but a life of faith at times trims us back. Sometimes we feel loss as part of denying self to follow Christ. There is a sobriety to a well-tended vineyard as well as a sense of permanence, order and attention.

Vines in winter, with their branches cut back, look very different from those at harvest, weighed down with leaves and ripe fruit. At times we might feel like bare, brittle twigs. Dormant times are necessary periods of rest in preparation for growth. In his 950 years Noah would have learned the rhythm of those times.

May we learn the grace of bearing fruit in our Vinedresser's time.

Lord, let me share that grace of thine
Wherewith thou didst sustain
The burden of the fruitful vine,
The gift of buried grain.
Who dies with thee, O Word divine,
Shall rise and live again.
Albert Orsborn (SASB 512)

41

In the Midst

'Sons were also born to Shem, whose older brother was Japheth;
Shem was the ancestor of all the sons of Eber' (v. 21).

Noah's middle son, Shem, carried the line of promise forward. Eber was his great-grandson. We're told the 'sons of Eber' means the offspring of Abraham or the Hebrew people. I wondered how Shem's wife would portray their encounters.

To bump into a mountain dock
watch a grey water world sink
and ours resurface,
to step out of the ark
breathe new air
stand firm on dry rock
hear song of bird and brook.
To worship God on peaks,
tangy smoke scenting my hair
His 'never again' pulsing my heart
his lucent bow sign blushing the sky.

This is not the end
just a pause in the mist
before we eight try again
to live forward in obedience to him.

Two years post-flood
when everything was growing back
Noah's middle son and wife,
I mean centenarian Shem and I,
birthed a boy, Arphaxad* –
healer, releaser –
he's our first,
yet in the middle too as
Adam's offspring ten removed,
and Abraham's forefather by ten.

But there is more.
Our line forecasts
Mary's
Son Jesus,
Crusher of Satan
Saviour of our world
Ruler of the next
Enthroned
encircled by emerald bow**
eternal Alpha and Omega.

*Genesis 11:10　　**Revelation 4:3

One Language

'Now the whole world had one language and a common speech' (v. 1).

The events in Genesis 11 were chronologically before those in Genesis 10. This is why chapter 11 speaks of one language. Noah's descendants migrated from the mountainous region of Ararat to the fertile more temperate plain of the Mesopotamia valley where they didn't have a ready supply of rocks for building. There must have been mud or clay available because they baked bricks. They used oil-based pitch for mortar. They seemed to work together to plan and build a city and the ambitious project of a skyscraper.

Various building projects are noted in Scripture. When done at God's direction and to bring honour to him, they were successful and approved. This one with a humanistic motive – 'to make a name for ourselves' (v. 4) – revealed self-sufficiency. We still build literal and metaphorical towers, at times capped with heliports. Does pride underlie some of our schemes?

The Godhead ('let us' of v. 7) decided that humankind's single tongue would accelerate their rebellion. The remedy was to confuse their language. Without clear communication, the project fell apart and the Lord scattered the people using the natural consequences of language differences.

Anyone who has struggled with a language knows the frustration of either forming entire sentences before speaking or trusting an elementary knowledge, speaking spontaneously and risking misunderstanding. Even though English is the dominant international language today, we smile at the anomalies within it. In the late 1800s a Jewish doctor from Warsaw attempted to develop a new language to be used as a second language to improve world understanding and peace – Esperanto. It has had limited success.

Pentecost (Acts 2) was the harbinger of the yet future day's reversal of Babel in a kingdom where believers from every nation, yet as one, will worship God in Christ.

Begin, my tongue, some heavenly theme,
Awake, my voice, and sing
The mighty works or mightier name
Of our eternal king.

Isaac Watts

43

En route

'Terah took his son Abram, his grandson Lot son of Haran, and his daughter-in-law Sarai, the wife of his son Abram, and together they set out from Ur of the Chaldeans to go to Canaan. But when they came to Haran, they settled there' (v. 31).

We move from primeval to patriarchal history and will pause in our journey through Genesis after introducing Abram. As we read names in the genealogy we notice that the life spans seem shorter than before. Women are not usually mentioned individually, but we see the names of Sarai and Milcah.

Who moved from the large cosmopolitan city of Ur to Haran and why? Terah, his son Abram and wife Sarai, and grandson Lot were in the party. Terah could have been part of the migration that took place when Ur's dynasty was eclipsed. We don't hear about God's 'call' to Abram in Genesis until after they'd settled in Haran. But in Acts 7:2–4 Stephen indicates that Abram was called in Ur, so his initial call may have been the driving force in the family's migration. Some of the family, including Nahor and wife Milcah and her sibling Iscah, stayed behind. It was from Nahor's clan that both Isaac and Jacob would one day find wives.

If they set out to go to Canaan, why did they settle in Haran en route? Was it special to the family, since Terah had a son named Haran? Haran had been born and died in Ur. Perhaps Terah's home was originally Haran. Many of Terah's ancestors' names are similar to place names in the land of Aram where the city of Haran was located. Could the family have been seeking their roots? Or maybe Terah meant to go on to Canaan, but Haran was as far as he could manage at his age.

The group stayed in Haran until Terah died at the age of 205. They accumulated possessions and people there, so the wait was providential preparation. Now Abram was definitely the head of the itinerant family and ready to hear and obey God. Do we subscribe to costly obedience as well?

While place we seek, or place we shun,
The soul finds happiness in none;
But with my God to guide my way
'Tis equal joy to go or stay.
                    Jeanne de la Mothe Guyon,
                    trans. William Cowper

New Point of View

'So Abram left, as the LORD had told him; and Lot went with him. Abram was seventy-five years old when he set out from Haran' (v. 4).

Why did God call Abram? God purposed to bless Abram and Sarai with a relationship with himself, to bring the Saviour of the world through their family, and to give believers examples of faith and faithfulness, albeit through some times of failure and forgiveness.

What did God tell Abram to do? Separate himself from the familiar – his country, family, culture – and from what he deserved to inherit. He'd done this to some extent in moving from Ur to Haran, so he knew the challenge of uprooting his life.

Those who have served away from their homeland, birth language and customs know something of what God asked of Abram. We can handle gradual change but when we jumble all points of reference we feel out of sync and unable to find outlets of expression.

What did God promise Abram? The blessings of direction to a specific place, of becoming father of a great nation, of prosperity, of a great name, of becoming a blessing to others and of being the conduit through which the whole world would be blessed (in the Messiah).

So Abram left Haran. He obeyed God. He believed God. No doubt he gained new perspective and dependence on God with each step away from his recognisable comfort zone. When they finally arrived in Canaan, the Lord appeared to Abram with confirmation that this was the land of promise (Genesis 12:7). When we obey God and go where he directs, he will appear to us in the new unfamiliar place.

Abram's response was to build an altar – the first of many. In fact, we can trace Abram's steps in following God's leading by the altars he left behind. These would be permanent testimonies to the God he worshipped – even when his nomadic life kept him living in tents.

Pioneers

*'They will still bear fruit in old age, they will stay fresh and green,
proclaiming, "The LORD is upright; he is my Rock, and there is
no wickedness in him"' (vv. 14, 15).*

Abram started his trek from Haran into the unknown at the age of seventy-five (he lived to 175). Noah's call to embark on his uncharted voyage of faith came at the age of 600 (he lived to 950). Church history is full of ordinary people who responded to the call of our extraordinary God and found the quest invigorating, albeit demanding, especially when it involved moving far away.

Mary, born in Greece to British parents serving in the military, was fifteen when her father died in Canada. She returned to England for education, met the early-day Salvation Army and the Lord, and sensed a call to serve him as a Salvation Army officer. A couple of years after training she and another woman officer were allowed to be engaged to two officers the Founder sent to California to start the Army work there. The women followed a year later. After a nine-day voyage to New York and a nine-day train trip they arrived in San Francisco to marry the men. No time for a honeymoon, they were immersed in mission.

Mary and Henry eventually started Salvation Army work in Oregon too. Mary took a particular interest in the troubles of young women and opened the Army's first rescue home for girls in the USA in Ohio. As a widow, she continued to raise her eight children and to supervise women's social work from Chicago to Honolulu. A number of Mary Stillwell's descendants have been soldiers or officers in the Army up to the present day. Several have served overseas. Colonel Mary Stillwell was my mother's grandmother (she lived to 85).

Everyone's pilgrimage on earth in obedience to God, whether long or brief, well-known or anonymous, is significant and unique. Heaven will reveal myriad testimonies of God's grace. In retrospect we see the ripple effects of answering God's call.

———

To ponder:

'He is no fool who gives what he cannot keep to gain what he cannot lose.'
*Written at age twenty-two by Jim Elliot, missionary to indigenous
people of Ecuador, martyred at the age of twenty-eight*

Fairest Lord Jesus

The choirs and orchestra of St Olaf College in Northfield, Minnesota, USA, present an annual concert that traditionally ends with F. Melius Christiansen's poignant arrangement of 'Fairest Lord Jesus'. As we read the hymn this Sunday, we consider our Creator, 'For from him and through him and to him are all things. To him be the glory for ever! Amen' (Romans 11:36).

> Fairest Lord Jesus,
> Lord of all nature,
> O thou of God and man the Son;
> Thee will I cherish,
> Thee will I honour,
> Thou my soul's glory, joy and crown.
>
> Fair are the meadows,
> Fairer the woodlands,
> Robed in the blooming garb of spring;
> Jesus is fairer,
> Jesus is purer,
> Who makes the woeful heart to sing.
>
> Fair is the sunshine,
> Fairer the moonlight,
> And all the twinkling starry host;
> Jesus shines brighter,
> Jesus shines purer
> Than all the angels heaven can boast.
>
> Beautiful Saviour,
> Lord of the nations,
> Son of God and Son of man,
> Glory and honour,
> Praise, adoration,
> Now and for evermore be thine.
>
> *Anonymous*

Belief in Action

The Letter of James

Introduction

Have you avoided the book of James? I admit that at times I've passed by the short Epistle. Do we wonder, as Martin Luther once did, whether we need its focus on works? In fact this brief book tells us how the faith of the gospel should be translated into daily life – a primer for practical holiness and support. Biblical faith always acts. In half the verses James calls hearers to actions that spring from right motives.

Since it dates to about AD 50, the letter of James was probably one of the first New Testament books written. Most people who had seen the risen Christ would have still been living then. The book was accepted from an early date only by some of the churches – probably as a result of being addressed to Jews of the Eastern dispersion.

James's admonition to accept whatever station transient life brings would have been understood by the exiled readers who may have known both extremes.

But it's interesting that James needed to remind his readers to be inclusive since the dispersed recipients would themselves have known the frustration of exclusion. Might they have reacted to their treatment and needed correction? We don't know, but the reminder is still relevant nearly 2,000 years later.

Most reading in the ancient world was done aloud. The letter of James appears to have been meant to be read aloud in public, perhaps as a sermon or vivid lecture. He uses similes and metaphors and alludes to passages from a score of Old Testament books. Some parts of James's teaching resemble John the Baptist's whom he probably heard preach. Other passages parallel Jesus' Sermon on the Mount. The Epistle differs from other Epistles in style (no concluding benediction or personal references, for example).

We will dip into this Epistle and find that James passionately promotes the completeness of a salvation by faith which results in evident holy living, while he encourages the mature believer for life's trials.

Bearing with Grace

'James, a servant of God and of the Lord Jesus Christ, To the twelve tribes scattered among the nations: Greetings' (v. 1).

In the New Testament there are several men named James – a form of the Hebrew name, Jacob. The author is generally accepted to be James the brother of Jesus. Although he was raised in the same home with Jesus, he apparently did not become a believer until after the resurrection. However, James (sometimes called 'James the Just') proved to be a faithful follower. He was martyred for his faith.

Unlike Paul's letters to specific churches he founded during his missionary journeys, the book of James is known as one of the general epistles. It was written to a general audience rather than to a specific congregation. It was written to dispersed Jewish Christians by a leader of the Jewish section of the Church which was centred in Jerusalem, so has distinct Jewish flavour and symbolism yet universal application.

At the start James refers to himself as a servant or bondservant of God. This familiar Old Testament phrase means 'worshipper'. James adds the New Testament element, 'and of the Lord Jesus Christ'. When Peter miraculously escaped from prison and told the astonished believers at Mary's house to tell the others about it, he mentioned James specifically. James lets others call him a pillar in the Church or the Lord's brother but identifies himself as a worshipper of Jesus.

We're told that the word 'greetings' could be 'hail' and literally means 'rejoice' or 'joy'. That ties in to the next verse: 'Consider it pure joy, my brothers'. James continues to link verses by repetition of principal words such as 'perseverance', 'lack', 'ask' and 'doubt'.

The heart of this opening passage is the believer's maturity or completeness of faith. For a life of trial he offers encouragement to steadfastness. The trials of many kinds common to all may involve mistreatment by others, wrenching loss, sickness, disappointment, stress, a combination of these and more.

Such testing brings pain but can also develop Christlike character as our muscles of commitment work hard in life's challenges. It is demanding work, but we are promised help: 'So we say with confidence, "The Lord is my helper; I will not be afraid. What can man do to me?"' (Hebrews 13:6).

Wisdom of God

'If any of you lacks wisdom, he should ask God, who gives generously to all without finding fault, and it will be given to him' (v. 5).

Trials are inevitable and sometimes numerous. How we bear them can be a testimony of our love for God. But how can we comprehend trials this way? It takes wisdom. So James tells us to ask God for that wisdom.

As a leader in the Early Church, James would know the value of seeking God's wisdom and receiving it. He presided at the Council of Jerusalem when the difficult question about imposing Jewish regulations on Gentile believers came to a head. After Peter, Barnabas and Paul defended the position of grace, James had the final word.

It may have been James who composed the letter sent to the new Christians in Antioch. (There are only two instances in the New Testament when the word 'greetings' is used – the council's letter and the book of James.) James would have been familiar with the book of Proverbs and its focus on wisdom. His contemporary, the apostle Paul, calls Christ the power and wisdom of God (1 Corinthians 1:24) and says that all the treasures of wisdom and knowledge are hidden in Christ (Colossians 2:3).

Wisdom for life isn't given in a moment, but the Enabler of wise choices is a promised gift from God if we ask for his presence. What is the wisdom for which a follower of Christ should ask? Jesus tells us in Luke 11:13: 'If you then, though you are evil, know how to give good gifts to your children, how much more will your Father in heaven give the Holy Spirit to those who ask him!'

―――――――

To pray:

> Holy Spirit! Promised Presence fall on me.
> Holy Spirit! Make me all I long to be.
> Holy Spirit! Holy Spirit!
> Give your power to me, O Holy Spirit.
> *John Gowans*[3]

Giver of All Good

'Every good and perfect gift is from above, coming down from the Father of the heavenly lights, who does not change like shifting shadows' (v. 17).

In verse 12 James refers again to the trials he spoke about in verses 2–4. This time he calls the one who perseveres 'blessed'. Does it remind us of the closing Beatitudes in Matthew 5:10–12? We can see a number of parallels between the Sermon on the Mount and the Epistle from James. He knew those teachings of Christ well. Reward comes to those who stand the test of trials.

But trials are not the same as temptations. If we excuse sin by blaming God for enticing us to do evil, we deny both God's holy character and his costly plan of redemption to destroy sin. We are drawn away by our own wrong desires when, like Eve, we choose to consider the enticing lies of Satan as viable options to God's commands.

This starts in the mind long before it is seen in actions. Jesus tells us that entertaining thoughts of evil is tantamount to sin (Matthew 5:21–30). The cumulative effect of a life of wilful sin is death (James 1:15). If we have succumbed to temptation, let us turn back to God swiftly, repent of sin, request forgiveness through Christ and know the Spirit's restoration of our hearts.

James warns the reader not to suppose that anything connected with evil could come from God. God, the source of all good things, gives only what is good. He is more dependable and unchanging than the sun, moon and stars he created to give us essential light for life. There is never an eclipse of his illumination and blessing beaming toward us. God is entirely dependable and we can approach him confidently.

Salvationist songwriter Frederick G. Hawkes may speak for us when he prays for a restful mind amidst tempests, a trustful mind when assailed by doubts and fears, an earnest mind to serve others to God's glory, a steadfast mind to endure to the end and a thankful mind to praise Christ with his whole being. Then with assurance he sums up his requests and entreats God:

> Great giver of all good,
> This priceless gift impart,
> On me this blessing now bestow,
> Fill thou my longing heart.

My Word

*'He chose to give us birth through the word of truth, that we
might be a kind of firstfruits of all he created' (v. 18).*

In several translations verse 18 is followed by 'so then' or 'wherefore'. In other
words, since the Word brought us to God, we need to be guided by the Holy
Spirit through the Word to progress as believers. Sensitivity to the truth of the
Word unites the instructions of verses 19–27.

Welcome the Word. 'Make a soil of humble modesty for the Word which roots
itself inwardly with power to save your souls' (v. 21, *JMT*).

Act on the Word. 'Do not merely listen to the word, and so deceive yourselves.
Do what it says' (v. 22).

When James instructs us to bridle our tongues (v. 26), we see that he views
speech as seriously as Jesus did when he said, 'For out of the overflow of the heart
the mouth speaks' (Matthew 12:34). Life teaches us to be more circumspect, to
learn to listen more attentively, but has any of us completely managed our words?
A heart full of love and a tongue that expresses it is pure religion.

Compassion in action follows religion marked by gracious speech. Care for the
most helpless (v. 27). Have a heart for the marginalised. The Early Church faced
its first social justice issue – discrimination. The Greek-speaking Jewish widows
received less food than others. The Church not only chose godly men to oversee
the more equitable distribution; they chose deacons with Greek names. They
showed Spirit-led wisdom in preserving the dignity of the neglected. When we
fold in the excluded, do we demonstrate respect for their worth?

Finally James tells us to keep unspotted from the world (v. 27). The world's
values can seep into our lives unnoticed. Are we intentional in the way we spend
our time and what we allow to feed our minds? Self-discipline creates spaces in
our lives for the Word to speak and the Spirit to work.

We pray with Harry Anderson:

> I give my heart to thee,
> Thy dwelling-place to be;
> I want thee ever in my heart;
> O live thy life in me!
> (*SASB* 455)

The Rule that's Spot On

'Speak and act as those who are going to be judged by the law that gives freedom, because judgment without mercy will be shown to anyone who has not been merciful. Mercy triumphs over judgment!' (vv. 12, 13).

James admonishes us not to try mixing faith in Christ with favouritism (v. 1). There is a certain justice in honouring people's service, character or faithfulness, but not in judging by externals. Favouritism disheartens and creates distance. It sends the message that such things as a person's appearance, wealth, rank, intelligence, musical ability, social graces, class, education or fitness matter unduly.

James points out that people God has chosen have often been those unnoticed by the world (v. 5). Paul wrote in similar vein:

> Brothers, think of what you were when you were called. Not many of you were wise by human standards; not many were influential; not many were of noble birth. But God chose the foolish things of the world to shame the wise; God chose the weak things of the world to shame the strong. (1 Corinthians 1:26, 27)

The best plan is to follow Jesus' example. He cared for the rich as well as siding with the forgotten and excluded. He knew poverty and brought good news to the poor. He treated women with dignity and wasn't afraid to mix with outsiders – whether outcast by disease or nationality. He was neither impressed nor revolted by anyone. He welcomed everyone. Christ welcomed us! As Christians we'll want to find new ways to welcome everyone.

As he did in chapter 1, James refers to the law that gives freedom and shows mercy (James 2:12, 13). What is that law, that rule that's always spot on? He says it's what Jesus replied when asked what the greatest commandment was: '"Love the Lord your God with all your heart and with all your soul and with all your mind" . . . And the second is like it: "Love your neighbour as yourself"' (Matthew 2:37, 39).

He drew a circle that shut me out –
Heretic, rebel, a thing to flout.
But love and I had the wit to win:
We drew a circle that took him in.
                    Edwin Markham
(an American who lived 1852–1940)

Visible Faith

*'You see that a person is justified by what he does and
not by faith alone' (v. 24).*

Do we sense contradiction between a gospel of faith and one of works, between Paul's letter to the Romans and James's letter? Actually the writers respected each other and their messages are complementary. Paul's words about saving faith are from a divine perspective and James's words about serving faith are from a human perspective. One is the seed and the other the fruit.

James does not put works above faith, but claims that only through righteous works can we see faith in action. In verse 14 James objects to counterfeit faith: 'Now what use is it, my brothers, for a man to say he "has faith" if his actions do not correspond with it? Could that sort of faith save anyone's soul?' (*JBP*).

After his illustration about the futility of wishing people well without doing anything to feed or clothe them, James replies to the objection someone might raise that one doesn't have to have both faith and deeds. Faith will do. James will have none of it. Belief in one God only puts us in league with demons, he says: 'So you believe that there is one God? That's fine. So do all the devils in hell and shudder in terror!' (v. 19, *JBP*).

James invokes Old Testament authority by making reference to individuals in Jewish history who showed faith in action. It was what Abraham believed *and* what he did that mattered. One completed the other. It was what Rahab believed *and* what she evidenced that mattered.

Our impulse to show love comes from our faith in Christ. God must delight in the variety of creative ways Christians have found to express faith in action. What more could our obedient faith produce?

Gracious Lord, thy grace apply,
Both to save and sanctify;
All my life wilt thou control,
Calmly ordering the whole,
That the world may ever see
Christ, and only Christ, in me.
  Colin Fairclough (SASB 479)

A Hymn to Christ the King

How fearsome and far
The Universe runs!
Who sees every star?
Who numbers new suns?
Our Christ is the King
Of unthinkable space,
And so we dare sing
Of his goodness and grace.

Strange secrets of life
New knowledge can tell
Amazing the strife
Of microbe and cell!
Our Christ is the King
Of the tiniest flower:
And so we dare sing
Of his goodness and power.

The last and the least
May answer his call:
'My Father's good feast
Is open to all.'
To ruin and shame him
They nailed him on high:
And now we acclaim him
For daring to die.

That terror is past –
When sin did its worst
He'll rule at the last,
Who reigned at the first,
The Lord of all years
That are coming to birth
As laughter and tears
Grow together on earth.

Dear Father, whose might
And mercy agree,
Your Word is our light,
So set us all free
To love and to labour,
To praise and to pray:
And share with our neighbour
The Christ of today.

John Coutts[4]

Master Control

'But the wisdom that comes from heaven is first of all pure;
then peace-loving, considerate, submissive, full of mercy and
good fruit, impartial and sincere' (v. 17).

In today's passage James more fully develops the thought he introduced in chapter 1 about being quick to listen and slow to speak. Tongue control is both the evidence and the means of spiritual maturity. Good comes from a controlled tongue and harm from an uncontrolled tongue far out of proportion to the number of words or size of the tongue.

James moves on naturally into advice about a talking profession, teaching. He counsels his readers not to presume to teach because of the liability of those who instruct others to be judged by what they teach others. Perhaps he also remembered Jesus' words: 'A student is not above his teacher, but everyone who is fully trained will be like his teacher' (Luke 6:40).

Were early Christians too eager to be masters? Was Christ's imminent return their urgency? In some cultures it takes at least ten years of apprenticeship before one can master an art or skill enough to teach others. At the least, James warns against taking on the role of spiritual life coaching lightly. If we do what we can to guide others it should not be for prestige or to act like an authority.

We can easily visualise James's illustrations from nature: bits in the mouths of horses, rudders on wind-driven ships, or tiny sparks setting whole forests ablaze. We understand the point: there is great power for good or ill in small things – especially the tongue. Besides its wide-range influence on others, the tongue can corrupt its owner. Humans can tame many animals, but taming the tongue is humanly impossible.

We might restrain our speech, but that isn't the same thing. Speech may only be a small part of the use of what the tongue signifies. Words form our thoughts, plans, imaginings and reactions. What we say is an index of our hearts: 'For out of the overflow of the heart the mouth speaks' (Matthew 12:34).

Is there praise and cursing out of the same mouth? This should not be (James 3:10). The source from which words spring and actions flow must be purified. Since James writes to believers in Christ he confidently states the remedy – seeking the Master's control and pure wisdom.

Pure Hearts

' *"Blessed are the pure in heart, for they will see God"* ' *(Matthew 5:8).*

James has written of pure joy, pure religion and pure wisdom. They all stem from a pure source, purity of heart to which he again refers in chapter 4. William Booth's book, *Purity of Heart*, explains what that is:

> In short, to be pure in soul signifies deliverance from all and everything which the Lord shows you to be opposed to his holy will. It means that you not only possess the ability to live the kind of life that he desires, but that you actually do live it.

Booth details what purity means and why it is important for every believer. After giving biblical and contemporary examples of the blessing, he concludes with advice about keeping it once received. He says that to keep the blessing we should pray (especially at regular hours), read and study the Bible, read books on holiness that will encourage us and be constantly watchful.

He concludes:

> If from any cause whatever you should lose the assurance that the blood of Jesus cleanses you; or if, more melancholy still, you should lose the blessing of purity, fly at once to your Saviour's feet, confess your wrongdoing, give yourself up again to the full service of your Lord, and once more plunge in the fountain opened for sin and uncleanness; and then, profiting by the sorrow and disappointment of your fall, start afresh to live the life of faith in a purifying Saviour.[5]

It's timeless advice as we begin the Lenten season tomorrow.

O for a heart to praise my God,
A heart from sin set free,
A heart that always feels the blood
So freely spilt for me.

A heart in every thought renewed,
And full of love divine;
Perfect and right, and pure and good,
A copy, Lord, of thine.

Thy nature, gracious Lord, impart,
Come quickly from above;
Write thy new name upon my heart,
Thy new best name of love.

Charles Wesley

For Lent

'Humble yourselves before the Lord, and he will lift you up' (v. 10).

Lent is one of the oldest observations in the Christian calendar. Although its length and starting date have changed through the years, the purpose has remained self-examination demonstrated by self-denial in preparation for Easter. Some churches use particular colours and sombre decorations during the season. Others follow prescribed disciplines.

One year I was challenged to participate in forty days of prayer and fasting. The prayer part was no problem. It would require extra time, but I should accent prayer, and would. But fasting? What could I do without? Food was out of the question since a medical condition limited my diet. TV-watching could go, but it wouldn't be much of a sacrifice. I prayed about the 'fasting' part.

When the answer came, it seemed so simple and obvious: 'Don't focus on subtracting, try *adding*!' So for forty days I added my chosen discipline and cooperated with the spirit of the Lenten emphasis. Wasn't Jesus' call to come, take up my cross and follow him largely an act of addition? Aren't we told to add to our faith goodness, knowledge, self-control, perseverance, godliness, brotherly kindness and love (2 Peter 1:5–7)?

F. W. Boreham tells the story of a pilot of an early-day aircraft and a rat. In mid-air the pilot heard gnawing behind him and thought with horror of the damage the teeth of a large rodent could do. Disaster might ensue. What could he do? He determined to soar. Rats weren't made for high altitudes. The pilot kept the plane climbing until he found breathing difficult. The gnawing stopped. In the added altitude the rat was suffocated by the rare air.

Sorting out, getting down to basics, simplifying our lives may be good advice for possessions and time. A decaffeinated, sugar-free, low-fat 'lite' diet may help our health. But when it comes to spiritual disciplines, consider trying a full-flavoured, costly, caring faith and focus on things that lift souls heavenward – yours and others.

To pray:

Ask the Lord if there is something he wants you to *add* for Lent.

Don't Assume

'Instead, you ought to say, "If it is the Lord's will, we will live and do this or that"' (v. 15).

James addresses businessmen, people engaged in making money. Their sin was not in planning but in failing to consider God in their plans. When they declared their plans brashly, they presumed the future to be predictable and within their control. It's another form of pride. It assumes what no one can, that we have tomorrow; that we are sole directors of our lives and that we can do whatever we set out to do.

James says we don't know about tomorrow (v. 14). A friend of mine who was looking forward to retirement in several years said she was learning to not count the days but to appreciate the blessings of each day. James would concur.

Not only are we not sovereign, our existence is relatively brief. James compares us with a transient mist. Not a gratifying correlation. What does mist or fog amount to? With global water shortages, scientists are exploring harvesting the fog. Still, it takes millions of fog droplets to form a drop of water, never mind a glass of water.

Impermanence and brevity of life can be used as an excuse for grabbing pleasure or for hopeless resignation. James advises neither. Rather our mortality should give us a sense of life's preciousness and God's sovereignty. Our attitude should acknowledge his will in our plans. Are we careless here? James considers the arrogance of presumptuousness serious enough to tie in a warning in the final verse of the chapter: 'Anyone, then, who knows the good he ought to do and doesn't do it, sins' (James 4:17).

If we sense guilt here, what can we do? We can turn to the Lord and pray with the psalmist:

Who can understand his errors? Cleanse me from secret faults. Keep back your servant also from presumptuous sins; let them not have dominion over me. Then I shall be blameless, and I shall be innocent of great transgression. Let the words of my mouth and the meditation of my heart be acceptable in your sight, O LORD, my strength and my Redeemer. (Psalm 19:12–14, *NKJV*)

When Gain is Loss

'This is how it will be with anyone who stores up things for himself but is not rich toward God' (Luke 12:21).

On the heels of speaking to merchants set on doing business without including God in their plans, James indicts unjust rich landowners. Why? Perhaps his warning to the rich is also a roundabout way of encouraging the poor or keeping them from envying the rich. He isn't against wealth, but opposes what a life of selfish hoarding can do to the hoarder and to those disadvantaged by it. The selfish use of wealth allows for a life of luxury and pleasure. But soft living leads to flabby hearts and insensitivity to others' needs.

What testifies against ill-gotten or self-indulgent gain? Rotten money, moth-eaten clothes, rusty metals or their modern equivalents of worthless currency, jumbled wardrobes, tarnished silver and a burgeoning self-storage industry.

Wealth acquired by exploiting others cries out. Offences against the innocent shout for justice and only increase the guilt of the oppressor. The Lord hears and knows. Does James sound like an Old Testament prophet (Isaiah 5)? His Jewish readers would understand his allusions and warnings.

It's been said that when shipwreck happens and passengers are adrift on lifeboats, values turn upside down (or right side up). People who flaunted gold clamour instead for oranges.

In Luke 12 Jesus tells a parable to warn of the insidiousness of greed. A rich man had such a good harvest that he didn't have room for it all. Was his solution to share it? No, he built more storage barns and revelled in his wealth, feeling self satisfied about the years ahead. But he died that night. Our sobering key verse concludes the lesson.

Isaac Watts offers proper perspective of what is most valuable for a Christian:

> When I survey the wondrous cross
> On which the Prince of Glory died,
> My richest gain I count but loss,
> And pour contempt on all my pride.

Resolute in Patience and Prayer

*'You also be patient. Establish your hearts, for the coming
of the Lord is at hand' (v. 8, NKJV).*

It takes a patient gardener to grow asparagus or rhubarb, since they are not harvested until the second or third year of growth. James says believers should learn from the farmer who is patient for the crops and for the rains (v. 7). A farmer in Palestine would depend on the autumn and spring rainy seasons to make the earth workable and ripen the harvest.

Besides being patient, James says we should firmly fix our hearts. The word used for 'establish' in our key verse is the same as used in Luke 9:51 when Jesus set his face to go toward Jerusalem and all that awaited him there. He was resolute. James uses the same word to tell us to steel our hearts to endure.

As we come to the end of the Epistle we see that James revisits several themes. James started his book with a call to steadfastness under trial and finishes with a call to patience and longsuffering (5:7, 8). He reminds us of how blessed we consider those who practised both (5:10, 11), then adds that the coming of the Lord should be the Christian's incentive.

Another tie between the opening and closing passages is prayer. In chapter 1 James urges prayer in seeking wisdom for staying the course. In chapter 5 he encourages prayer again in every situation, not just for our needs, but for others' too. Answers to prayer become the basis of confidence for further prayer, such as in Elijah's case (vv. 17, 18). Prayer creates the opportunity for grace to work.

James's emphasis on controlling the tongue resurfaces in this concluding chapter too. This time he counsels not to grumble against each other and not to say more than yes or no. There is no need for exaggeration or oaths, no need to invoke God's name carelessly or to use unnecessary expletives, misleading words or duplicity. We can be wholehearted with God and humankind and practise devotion to the truth with what we say because it's what is in our hearts.

To ponder:

How would I describe my belief in action?

Lord, Teach Us to Pray

Prayer is the soul's sincere desire
Uttered or unexpressed,
The motion of a hidden fire
That trembles in the breast.

Prayer is the burden of a sigh,
The falling of a tear,
The upward glancing of an eye
When none but God is near.

Prayer is the simplest form of speech
That infant lips can try;
Prayer the sublimest strains that reach
The majesty on high.

Prayer is the contrite sinner's voice
Returning from his ways,
While angels in their songs rejoice
And cry: Behold, he prays!

Prayer is the Christian's vital breath,
The Christian's native air,
His watchword at the gates of death;
He enters Heaven with prayer.

O thou by whom we come to God,
The life, the truth, the way!
The path of prayer thyself hast trod:
Lord, teach us how to pray!

James Montgomery

For a billion people the Bible is a luxury they cannot afford. Please pray for the 140 national Bible Societies working to make the Bible available and affordable to those who long for its life-changing message.

World Day of Prayer will be observed on Friday 6 March. Christians in Papua New Guinea have prepared resources on the theme 'In Christ, there are many members, yet one body'. Please pray for the people of Papua New Guinea.

Partnerships In Ministry

(A series by guest writers Lieutenant-Colonels Richard and Janet Munn)

Introduction

> A high-powered husband–wife team can be a formidable political force in the firm. (Alvin Toffler[6])

Couples in ministry – it's one of the truly distinctive features of The Salvation Army. For many in the ranks it's all we've ever known. For people in other traditions, it can be either powerfully attractive or distinctly uncomfortable.

What are we to make of such a scenario? Is there a biblical motif that can provide solid empowerment in this age of both feminism and patriarchy? The next four weeks highlight four biblical couples – Adam and Eve, Esther and Xerxes, Mary and Joseph, Priscilla and Aquila – to glean what they represent *together* in ministry.

Hold on! You might be surprised at the insights that surface.

Richard Munn was born in London, England, and spent the first ten years of his life in the Congo, where his parents were missionary teachers for The Salvation Army. Janet grew up in Massachusetts, USA, her father being a pastor in the Church of the Nazarene. For several summers during their student years they both worked at The Salvation Army's Camp Wonderland, Massachusetts. It was this experience, serving underprivileged children, that God used to birth a vision for ministry. They were married in 1980 and have two young adult children.

In 1987 they were commissioned as officers in The Salvation Army, USA Eastern Territory. Following corps (church) work in Camden, New Jersey, and youth ministry in Massachusetts, the Munns were corps officers (church ministers) in Manchester, Connecticut, and then divisional leaders in Northern New England. For nearly three years they served at USA Eastern Territorial Headquarters as Secretary for Programme and Ambassador for Prayer and Spiritual Formation respectively.

In July 2008 the Munns were transferred to London. Richard was appointed Principal of The Salvation Army's International College for Officers and Centre for Spiritual Life Development, and Secretary for International Ecumenical Relations; Janet became Associate Principal of the International College for Officers and Centre for Spiritual Life Development, and Secretary for Spiritual Life Development.

Richard graduated from St Luke's College, Exeter (BEd) and from Asbury Theological Seminary (MDiv). He also received a Doctor of Ministry degree from Gordon Conwell Theological Seminary, Massachusetts. Janet is a graduate of Asbury College (BA) and received a Master of Arts in Leadership and Ministry from Greenville College, Illinois.

(1) Adam and Eve
'We Really Do Need Each Other'

'"It is not good for the man to be alone"' (v. 18).

A popular song suggests: 'Let's start at the very beginning. It's a very good place to start.' So let's do that in this matter of 'partnerships in ministry'. The very best place to start is surely the story of creation itself, with that archetypal partnership, Adam and Eve.

By any standards, in the very beginning Adam has it made in Eden. Every creature comfort is provided. However, in spite of this opulence, Adam is strangely unfulfilled. He remains alone. He is only half the story. Can it be that the image of God in him yearns for the presence of a counterpart, without whom there is no fulfilment?

Even before the creation of Adam, we can assert with some confidence that there is perfect community within the Trinity. The 'co-equality' between the persons connotes the polar opposite of isolation and loneliness. So yes, Adam needs a partner to perfectly complete the image of God in him.

This is a powerfully primeval force that remains undiminished through the subsequent centuries and across every conceivable culture. It is reflected in Paul's insightful pronouncement, 'In the Lord . . . woman is not independent of man, nor is man independent of woman' (1 Corinthians 11:11).

Marriage is the primary means by which male and female empower each other. Weathering currently trendy alternatives, this ancient bond is as popular as ever. 'It does no harm to tell ourselves again that in fact happy and successful marriages outnumber those that eventually break down', General Shaw Clifton has written.

I believe in marriage. Do you? I stand against the forces that assault its value and beauty in our world. I esteem its incalculable worth and grieve over its wounds.

Today, meditate upon the marriages that have influenced you for good: your own, those in your family of origin, those modelled around you – both now, and those in your youth. Pray thanks for them; if married, pray together; speak health into those that the Lord reveals to you.

'Help! I Need Somebody!'

'"I will make a helper suitable for him"' (Genesis 2:18).

'Help, you know I need someone!' intoned the cheery Beatles in the mid-1960s, unwittingly replicating a quite theologically accurate heart cry of Adam in Eden. With God's provision of Adam's 'helper' there is again an emphasis of the man and the woman as social beings. The word communicates the concept of a 'counterpart' and the accurate translation suggests 'like his counterpart, corresponding to him'.

Far from implying *helper* as an assistant – as in 'my pretty little assistant' – the word instead illustrates the shortfall and vulnerability of man when bereft of woman in Eden. Shockingly, God seems to provide Adam with a 'rescuer'. For instance, reference is made to God himself as the 'helper' of Israel.

Here, however, the concept describes a mutually beneficial relationship, one without rank or position. As writer Ellen White puts it in *Patriarchs and Prophets*,

> Eve was created from a rib taken from the side of Adam, signifying that she was not to control him as the head, nor to be trampled under his feet as an inferior, but to stand by his side as an equal, to be loved and protected by him.[7]

It just may be that you are being indifferent to the person God has sent alongside to complement you. Men, you have to face an ancient temptation, thinking that women are inherently subservient. Women, you have to counter docility. Don't believe it for a second.

Maybe the Beatles got it right – we all need to change our minds and open up some doors.

Imago Dei

'So God created man in his own image, in the image of God he created him;
male and female he created them' (Genesis 1:27).

In Greek mythology Narcissus is renowned as the beautiful youth so besotted with himself that he unerringly gazes at his poolside reflection by the hour – ultimately to his doom. Written as a warning against self-infatuation, the truth is seemingly ignored by whole schools of thinking today. In the niche celebrity market it reigns supreme, the *a priori* for a star on Hollywood Boulevard. On a broader scale, the scientific primacy of human beings as inherently the source of ultimate truth betrays whopping self-adulation. In contrast, Christians attest to the conferred dignity of being created in the image of God – males and females, as precisely recorded in Genesis.

God determines to make 'man' (singular), but intriguingly refers to 'man' as 'them' (plural). 'Man', we learn, is a generic term for 'human beings' and encompasses both male and female. Thus, both man and woman are God's image-bearers. Femaleness pertains to the image of God as fully as maleness. The challenge for us seems to come in matching the espoused theory with the theory-in-use. The nub comes sneakily in the preceding verse: 'God said, "Let us make man in our image, in our likeness, and let them rule"' (Genesis 1:26).

If both men and women are made in the image of God, and if both are accorded rulership over the earth as an outcome of this sanctity, then both men and women, husbands and wives, are equally endowed with the capacity for leadership. The biblical record seems to point quite acutely against an 'old boys' mentality.

The missional implication for husband and wife partnerships is full of transforming potential: shared leadership, shared authority, shared public roles, mutual deference, interdependent creativity and a lot more.

Men: Is there a spouse close to you just waiting to flower, her sacred creative endowment muzzled by your erroneous theology? Women: Is there a spouse close to you just wilting under the pressure to produce alone, to always have the last word and the right answer?

Egalitarian Intimacy

*'The man and his wife were both naked, and they
felt no shame' (Genesis 2:25).*

From the marriage and ministry of William and Catherine Booth, thousands of Salvation Army couples through the decades and across cultures have an inspiring model to emulate. In fact, the egalitarian leadership model is a long-standing and unique facet of Salvation Army mission. Today, as dual-career marriages become culturally more normal this appears genuinely strategic as a point of connection. Quite simply, many Salvationists are part of a culture that appears to be increasingly more open to men and women leading together. Is there a biblical basis for this?

The Genesis creation narrative conveys the idea that man and woman are created to enjoy intimate community together. This is implicit in Genesis 1 and explicit in Genesis 2. Man is relieved from isolation and loneliness by the creation of woman. It is evident that this void could not be filled by the presence of animals. Startlingly, it is not even placated by the presence of God. A specifically female counterpart is the only antidote. The creation of Eve from Adam's rib reveals that God's intention is that she will be – unlike the animals – an entity equal to him.

God also creates the man and the woman with a capacity to care for and to love another human being. In this way God equips us to be like him. He creates in us his own capacity to love. The profound oneness in the original creation sets the standard for all marital relationships. Two become one. The one-flesh union expresses full personality. Two spirits express mutual relational commitment.

Emily and George Walther express this well in *Celebrating Our Partnership*:

> When we become one in the way the Lord intended, a new union takes place, and a new personality is formed – our couple personality, in which the whole is greater than the sum of the parts. That's true oneness, true intimacy, true and full partnership.[8]

Today, prayerfully bring your marriage before the Lord. How is your marital partnership a healthy witness for the gospel? What makes your 'couple personality' attractive? How can you more fully experience egalitarian intimacy?

He Shall Rule Over You!

*' "Your desire will be for your husband, and he will
rule over you"' (Genesis 3:16).*

In William Shakespeare's comedy *The Taming of the Shrew* the crux of the story centres on a man who marries a very fiery woman. The climax is a tour de force for the husband, as his wife meekly – and publicly – subjects herself to his authority. Triumph! Order restored, as God intended! In actuality it is yet another coup for heinous disintegration between the genders.

The sin of Adam and Eve catastrophically breaks the ideal Edenic relationship. God is almost vulnerably tender, but swiftly pronounces the penalties. For man, the punishment is toil of the earth. For woman, the punishment is increased pain in childbearing and a 'desire' for her husband that will be instead reciprocated with his 'rule over you' (Genesis 3:16).

Man now masters woman, as the earth masters man. Just as death and the toil of the earth – absent in Eden to this point – result from sin, so too does the pain of childbirth and the dominance of man over woman. Thus, both male dominance and death are antithetical to God's original intent in creation.

'He will rule over you' is not God's prescriptive will, any more than death may be regarded as God's will for humans, says theologian Gilbert Bilezikian. As a result of sin, the original relational harmony has degenerated into a horrible and disfigured mutation. The ugly intrusion of sin inflicts a devastating blow upon intimacy. Men and women are separated from God and each other.

While this is painful in any setting, the effect seems especially hurtful when subsequently promoted as God's will. This is epitomised with the egregious assertion that a woman is divinely mandated to function as subordinate to man. What excruciating perverseness! What diabolical injustice!

This is an ancient curse that needs to be ruthlessly countered. 'Husbands, love your wives, just as Christ loved the church and gave himself up for her', writes Paul (Ephesians 5:25). Beloved Salvationists, wade into this fight! Gender inequality is an evil worth assaulting.

Proto Euangelion Hope

'"I will put enmity between you and the woman, and between
your offspring and hers; he will crush your head, and you
will strike his heel"' (Genesis 3:15).

I recall sitting in a large Salvation Army gathering when a choreographed group began chanting 'Hope! Hope! Hope!' What particularly inspired me was the intensity of one of the participants, who I knew was enduring painful difficulties with her eldest child. In the middle of darkness she willed the light of hope.

Genesis 3:15 has a similarly prophetic capacity. It holds the first biblical promise of future redemption – *proto euangelion* – that someone will crush the satanic head. God's pronouncement contains the assurance of victory by the woman through her offspring. The passage is striking; it is a declaration of mercy, God's blessing on future generations is not removed after all.

Dotted throughout Scripture, glimpses of restored intimacy are subsequently revealed. They seem to be subtly placed – a hint here, a nuance there. For instance, the marital beauty of the couple described in Song of Songs surely reflects God's original Edenic intention. The energy of the poem is found in the intensity of the couple. Together they represent a formidable force.

The leitmotif is perfect: 'I am my beloved's, and my beloved is mine' (Song of Solomon 6:3, *KJV*). The verse links with Genesis 3:16 – 'Your *desire* will be for your husband, and he will rule over you.' Except now wife and husband relate and play innocently and with equal abandon. They are curious about each other; they please one another; they appreciate each other. The implication for couples is found not so much in the portrayal of joyful intimacy as in the complete absence of ugly domination, subjugation or manipulation.

This week, as we have surveyed the original couple, we have delighted in their potential and agonised at their sinful choices. We conclude with the gospel of hope; dare we imagine Song of Songs actually depicts Adam and Eve restored in heaven?

Assert this hope into your marriage; and the marriages of your parents, your children and your friends. Here is a promise for you: 'I [God] will repay you for the years the locusts have eaten' (Joel 2:25).

Delivered

O LORD, how many are my foes!
How many rise up against me!
Many are saying of me,
'God will not deliver him.'

Selah

But you are a shield around me, O LORD;
you bestow glory on me and lift up my head.
To the LORD I cry aloud,
and he answers me from his holy hill.

Selah

I lie down and sleep;
I wake again, because the LORD sustains me.
I will not fear the tens of thousands
drawn up against me on every side.

Arise, O LORD!
Deliver me, O my God!
Strike all my enemies on the jaw;
break the teeth of the wicked.

From the LORD comes deliverance.
May your blessing be on your people.

Selah

This week, on 10 and 11 March, Jews will celebrate Purim and remember God's deliverance of his people through Esther. They will read and re-enact the story from the book of Esther (recorded in chapter 9), delight in the outcome and eat special foods to commemorate the victory. How can Christians join in the spirit of celebration and thanksgiving for liberty? We can remember when God delivered us personally and praise him.

(2) Esther and Xerxes

What Does He See in Her?

*'But Esther had kept secret her family background and nationality just as
Mordecai had told her to do, for she continued to follow Mordecai's
instructions as she had done when he was bringing her up' (Esther 2:20).*

Jack Sprat could eat no fat, his wife could eat no lean,
And so between them both, you see, they licked the platter clean.
Nursery rhyme

Xerxes was a powerful man. Esther was a powerless girl. He was the king. She
was an orphan. He was royalty. She was an exile, a foreigner. He had advisers,
noblemen, servants. She had one living relative, also a foreigner in exile. He had a
harem. She was a virgin. He gave commands, pronounced edicts. She followed
orders, listened to counsel. He had strength. She had weakness.

He was manipulated by his advisers. She outsmarted his second-in-command.
He was ready to annihilate a whole group of people. She was willing to die so that
the people would live. He was impulsive, hot-tempered, self-centred. She was
discreet, self-controlled, self-sacrificing.

Her beauty attracted his attention and her wisdom directed his power. He
chose her from among many. She guided him to deliver the many. He brought her
from ordinariness, anonymity and insignificance to greatness, fame and influence.
She spared him from injustice, collusion and bloodguilt.

At first glance Esther seemed beneath Xerxes, too low in her social standing. In
the end she demonstrated wisdom, courage and cunning far beyond that of
Xerxes. Esther and Xerxes partnered together to save the Jewish exiles in Persia. To
accomplish that end they needed each other.

Christians in the New Testament are told not to be 'unequally yoked' with
unbelievers, and this is often applied to marriage – a Christian, some believe,
should not marry, be yoked together, with an unbeliever (2 Corinthians 6:14). Also
in the New Testament the Church is described as the Bride of Christ, the wife of
the Lamb (Revelation 21:9). How great is the inequality of this Bridegroom and
Bride? Yet Jesus is a holy man and he will marry a holy bride.

In the end we, the Church, will be equally yoked with our Bridegroom even as
we partner together to bring salvation to the world and establish a kingdom of
righteousness.

Who's the Fairest of Them All?

*'Then the king's personal attendants proposed, "Let a search be
made for beautiful young virgins for the king"' (v. 2).*

Everyone – male and female – takes part in a quest for beauty. Many seek it out in healthy ways through the enjoyment of a symphony, an art museum, a sunset, the laughter of a child, the face of a loved one. But some seek it in not-so-healthy ways, such as the estimated 10 million teenagers with eating disorders, who starve themselves trying to achieve the ideal 'beauty' they see portrayed in the popular media. Another 72 million people regularly view the 4.2 million pornographic websites in existence, seeking some perverse version of beauty.

The advisers to Xerxes, King of Persia in the fifth century BC, understood this universal hunger for beauty – to discover it, gaze at it, possess it. So, with Queen Vashti having been ousted from her position of honour, they make the suggestion to Xerxes that a search be made in every province of the Persian Empire for beautiful young unmarried women. They would search out beauty for the king. Not surprisingly the idea appealed to Xerxes.

Where does this hunger for beauty originate? Humans are created in the image of the One who is the source and fullness of perfect beauty, the Lord. He is thus described many times throughout Scripture, particularly with reference to his holiness. In fact the beauty of the Lord is so overwhelming that when humans get a glimpse of it they often pass out, faint or, in biblical language, 'fall at his feet as though dead'. That's some beauty!

How does your longing for beauty express itself? Join with the psalmist in holy pursuit:

O worship the LORD in the beauty of holiness: fear before him, all the earth. (Psalm 96:9, *KJV*)

One thing I ask of the LORD, this is what I seek . . . to gaze upon the beauty of the LORD and to seek him in his temple. (Psalm 27:4, *NIV*)

To ponder:

> Let the beauty of Jesus be seen in me,
> All his wonderful passion and purity,
> O thou Spirit divine, all my nature refine,
> Till the beauty of Jesus be seen in me.
> *Albert Orsborn (SASB, chorus 77)*

For Such a Time as This

' "Go, gather together all the Jews who are in Susa, and fast for me. Do not eat or drink for three days, night or day. I and my maids will fast as you do. When this is done, I will go to the king, even though it is against the law. And if I perish, I perish" ' (Esther 4:16).

The prophet Amos (Amos 5:13) as well as the apostle Paul (Ephesians 5:16) state that the times are evil. The men of Issachar in the Old Testament were described as those who understood the times in which they were living and knew what they needed to do (1 Chronicles 12:32). The apostle Paul reminds us that the Lord has prepared in advance good works for us to do (Ephesians 2:10). Evil times. Understanding the times. Doing the right work at the right time.

Esther was living in evil times. Haman had hatched a plan to annihilate Esther's people, all the Jews living in Persian exile. Mordecai was outraged, desperate, inconsolable, and presented Esther with the challenge to plead with the king for mercy on their behalf. Understanding the times, he further asserted that this was probably the very reason for which she had 'come to royal position' (Esther 4:14), one of influence with the king.

Esther was coming into her finest hour, the reason for her exalted status – for the sake of the salvation of others – vulnerable people, without access to the corridors of power. She was to become a voice for the voiceless. Esther demonstrated great love – a willingness to lay down her life for others.

This is the same love demonstrated in Jesus Christ. To express it is our daily calling as people of the Cross.

———

To ponder:

'From everyone who has been given much, much will be demanded; and from the one who has been entrusted with much, much more will be asked.'

(Luke 12:48)

'For whoever wants to save his life will lose it, but whoever loses his life for me will save it.'

(Luke 9:24)

'The Son of Man did not come to be served, but to serve, and to give his life as a ransom for many.'

(Matthew 20:28)

It's Not Lonely at the Top

'Esther had not revealed her nationality and family background, because Mordecai had forbidden her to do so' (Esther 2:10).

Do you sometimes feel that no one truly knows you,
And that no one understands or really cares?
Through his people, God himself is close beside you,
And through them he plans to answer all your prayers.

John Gowans (SASB 238)

Esther had become Queen of the Persian Empire, positioned for great influence. While she had clearly demonstrated wisdom and courage, she had not risen to that position or gained such influence on her own. Her relative Mordecai had taken responsibility for her life when she was an orphaned child and continued to visit Esther daily during the months that she was preparing to come before the king (Esther 2:11). Mordecai's wisdom and counsel guided her in childhood and throughout her life in the palace. The king's eunuch, Hegai, was also a source of advice and support for Esther during her period of preparation, and his assistance contributed to her ascension to the throne (Esther 2:8–9, 15).

Queen and king. Esther and Xerxes. The leaders of the empire. The enthroned ones. Yet both depended upon others, wittingly or unwittingly, to fulfil their role in God's great purposes during their moment in history.

Whatever our role or status in this world, none of us is self-made. We all have been influenced by others and continue to be dependent upon others even as others are dependent upon us. Although cultural influences might tell us we are self-sufficient, we are not. This mutual interdependence is a reflection of the Godhead – the Trinity, Father, Son and Spirit. It's not lonely at the top!

Are you in honest, trusting relationships with other Christians? Are you depending on others and being dependable for them? Are you seeking out authentic Christian community? Or are you trying to live privatised Christianity?

To ponder:

'For lack of guidance a nation falls, but many advisers make victory sure.'

(Proverbs 11:14)

Are You as Good as You Look?

'Now the king was attracted to Esther more than to any of the other
women, and she won his favour and approval more than any
of the other virgins. So he set a royal crown on her head and made
her queen instead of Vashti' (Esther 2:17).

As a little girl, my mother would dress me for church each week as though we were going to a wedding or gala event – pretty dress, bow in my hair, white gloves, black patent leather shoes, the works. Each week at church an elderly man would greet me with a smile, comment admiringly on my dress and then ask me, 'Jan, are you as good as you look?' It was a question that even in my earliest years brought conviction to my heart. I knew how selfish I was, how angry with my brother, how vain about my outfit. No, I was not as good as I looked, all dressed up on a Sunday morning.

Esther's physical appearance, her looks, were outstanding among the many in the king's harem. She was the favourite of Hegai, the eunuch in charge of the harem, so was the beneficiary of his personal beauty treatments for a full year and more. Esther looked good.

Yet chapter 5 of the book of Esther reveals to us courage and cunning, wisdom and wit on the part of the orphan-girl-become-queen. She heeds the counsel of her faithful adoptive father Mordecai. She makes the quality decision to risk her life for the sake of others rather than remain silent in the hopes of saving only herself. She cooks up a dinner plan in the palace and ushers in a revolution in the kingdom. In the end, it became apparent to all that Esther was as good as she looked. Probably better.

How about you? How does your inner life compare to your outer appearance, reputation or image?

To ponder:

'Charm is deceptive, and beauty is fleeting; but a woman who fears the LORD is to be praised.'   *(Proverbs 31:30)*

'Woe to you, teachers of the law and Pharisees, you hypocrites! You are like whitewashed tombs, which look beautiful on the outside but on the inside are full of dead men's bones and everything unclean.'   *(Matthew 23:27)*

'Blind Pharisee! First clean the inside of the cup and dish, and then the outside also will be clean.'   *(Matthew 23:26)*

The Great Reversal

*'So they hanged Haman on the gallows he had
prepared for Mordecai' (v. 10).*

'It ain't over till it's over' – so said Yogi Berra, baseball player for the New York Yankees, 1946–63.

The edict for the slaughter of the Jews had been distributed; the signet ring was on Haman's finger; the gallows had been built awaiting Mordecai's neck; dinner at the palace with the royal couple was planned for the evening. Things were looking great for Haman. Within a matter of days his immediate enemy Mordecai would be hanged, and all Mordecai's people, the Jews, would be annihilated. He was so close to taking the throne he could taste it.

In a day everything changed: the edict was reversed; the signet ring was on Mordecai's finger; Haman was hanged on the gallows he had built for Mordecai; and Mordecai was dining in the palace with the royal couple – so close to the throne he could taste it.

How could everything change so suddenly? The great reversal, the mighty deliverance of God's people, came about by means of ordinary people and extraordinary people partnering together with one another and with the Lord.

This was neither the first nor the last time there would be such a great reversal in a day. At the birth of Jesus Christ, in a day, everything changed. God had come to earth, had moved into the neighbourhood, and by what means? By means of ordinary human beings in partnership with Jesus himself. Good Friday, the murder of the Son of God, the Saviour of the World, the King of the Jews. All was darkness, despair, defeat. In a day, everything changed. Life conquered death, the grave was empty, heaven was opened. By what means? By God and humankind, by the God-Man offering his life for ours.

There are more great reversals happening every day. Do you want to be part of these miracles? By what means, you ask? By offering yourself in partnership with the Holy Spirit of the living God, to accomplish his will on earth.

To ponder:

'Who is like the Lord our God, the One who sits enthroned on high? . . . He raises the poor from the dust and lifts the needy from the ash heap; he seats them with princes, with the princes of their people.'

(Psalm 113:5, 7, 8)

Glory to God in the Highest

On this Sunday let us join the worldwide chorus of praise to the Lord and in his temple cry, 'Glory!'

Ascribe to the LORD, O mighty ones,
ascribe to the LORD glory and strength.
Ascribe to the LORD the glory due his name;
worship the LORD in the splendour of his holiness.

The voice of the LORD is over the waters;
the God of glory thunders,
the LORD thunders over the mighty waters.
The voice of the LORD is powerful;
the voice of the LORD is majestic.
The voice of the LORD breaks the cedars;
the LORD breaks in pieces the cedars of Lebanon.
He makes Lebanon skip like a calf,
Sirion like a young wild ox.
The voice of the LORD strikes
with flashes of lightning.
The voice of the LORD shakes the desert;
the LORD shakes the Desert of Kadesh.
The voice of the LORD twists the oaks
and strips the forests bare.
And in his temple all cry, 'Glory!'

The LORD sits enthroned over the flood;
the LORD is enthroned as King for ever.
The LORD gives strength to his people;
the LORD blesses his people with peace.

(3) Mary and Joseph
A Heart Condition

'"For he has been mindful of the humble state of his servant.
From now on all generations will call me blessed"' (v. 48).

Why her? Of all the women in the history of the Hebrew people, why Mary? Of all the women living in Nazareth, or in the vicinity of Galilee, why was she the one to conceive by the Holy Spirit and give birth to the Son of God?

Why him? Of all the men who could have filled the role, why Joseph? Of all the eligible bachelors, even among carpenters, why was he the one chosen to protect this mother and child, to receive angelic dreams and to help nurture throughout his childhood God-in-the-flesh?

There must have been many righteous Jews living in the area; lots of godly young Hebrew virgins and plenty of devout single Jewish men. Surely there were others who were equally devoted to the law of Moses, to the Jewish customs and ritual observance, and perhaps more articulate. But God looks at the heart, an alternately comforting and frightening thought. Comforting – God knows who we really are inside in a way no one else does. Frightening – God knows who we really are inside in a way no one else does.

A quality of heart that God highly esteems is humility and Mary bursts forth in song celebrating this: 'For he has been mindful of the *humble* state of his servant. From now on all generations will call me blessed . . . He has brought down rulers from their thrones but has lifted up the *humble*' (vv. 48, 52).

Mary recognised her own qualification for the job, her own heart condition – humility – and that God specialises in lifting up the humble. Joseph too – while we have no recorded hymn of praise from his lips, he demonstrated the humility of heart to submit to the will and Word of the Lord, to take a pregnant woman as his wife and to believe all was holy.

Jesus manifested the fullness of humility in human form. Perhaps he learned it in part through his parents' example. How can you humble yourself today? In what way can you take action in this and strike a blow to pride – the very thing God hates and the very essence of sin?

It's Not About You

'[Joseph] went and lived in a town called Nazareth. So was fulfilled
what was said through the prophets: "He will be called a Nazarene"'
(Matthew 2:23).

e·go·cen·tric – *adjective*, having or regarding the self as the centre of all things.

More often than not the star of the wedding seems to be the bride, with the
groom fulfilling his role as best supporting actor. This is even more the case
at the birth of a baby – it's mum and baby. Dad plays an important role, but clearly
a supporting one. This may never have been more so than in the story of the birth
of Jesus and the marriage of his mother and stepfather, Mary and Joseph. If ever a
wedding and a birth were not about the husband or father, it is in this story.

Joseph reverses his quiet divorce plans because of the angel's instruction.
Joseph, we presume, takes full financial and fatherly child-rearing responsibility
for this child, though not his own offspring. Even the name of the boy is chosen
by someone other than Joseph – God chose the name for him, Jesus.

Mary, the mother, gets special commendation from the angel Gabriel; angels
and shepherds are celebrating the birth of the child; the Magi came and saw 'the
child with his mother Mary' (Matthew 2:11); three more times in the early
chapters of Matthew's Gospel, Joseph's dedication is demonstrated by his diligence
in following orders for the sake of the mother and the baby.

Joseph is a prototype for us all. We are on this earth not to promote ourselves,
advance our own agendas or do as we please. When John the Baptist was asked to
explain why so many of his disciples were leaving him and following Jesus, he
replied: 'The bride belongs to the bridegroom. The friend who attends the bridegroom waits and listens for him, and is full of joy when he hears the bridegroom's
voice. That joy is mine, and it is now complete' (John 3:29).

Jesus eventually laid down his life for his Bride, even as his earthly father Joseph
lived his for his bride . . . and her son.

How can you live your life at the ready to respond to divine instruction, for the
sake of a vulnerable one such as a child? What does your personal calendar reveal
about your priorities? For whom are you living?

Mother of the Impossible

' "*For nothing is impossible with God*" ' (v. 37).

An angel visiting a teenager? A virgin conceiving? Impossible! Guidance from heaven through the dream of a carpenter? Impossible! Naïve newlyweds eluding the murderous plans of the conniving King Herod? Impossible! God becoming human? The uncreated God of the universe becoming a vulnerable human baby? Impossible!

The whole story, every detail, is a juxtaposition of the ordinary with the impossible. The path is strewn with ordinary – a teenager, conception, a carpenter, newlyweds, a baby. Nothing special there. Right alongside the ordinary is the impossible, the miraculous – angels, dreams and visions, laws of nature suspended, outrageous provision.

Of all the possibilities, why Mary to bear the Son of God? Perhaps because she heard the Word of the Lord and believed it – making her womb a fertile environment for the holy seed to be planted and grow there. An environment of faith. The environment of a heart that pleases God always attracts his favour. Scripture reminds us: 'And without faith it is impossible to please God, because anyone who comes to him must believe that he exists and that he rewards those who earnestly seek him' (Hebrews 11:6).

All the credit Abraham got was because of his faith. All the heroes listed in the eleventh chapter of Hebrews were heroes because of their faith. The absence of faith means God-pleasing is also absent. Alternately, the presence of faith delights God's heart. Hence, Gabriel's description that Mary was highly favoured must imply the presence of faith within her.

What has the Lord said to you? What word has the Spirit whispered in your heart? What is your response? How can you cultivate an environment of faith within, for the incorruptible seed of the Word of God to take root, flourish and bear much fruit?

Do whatever it takes – and you'll be blessed, highly favoured, with a life where the impossible is realised.

———

To ponder:

'Blessed is she who has believed that what the Lord has said to her will be accomplished!'

(Luke 1:45)

A Dreamy Couple

'When they had gone, an angel of the Lord appeared to Joseph in a dream. "Get up," he said, "take the child and his mother and escape to Egypt. Stay there until I tell you, for Herod is going to search for the child to kill him"'
(Matthew 2:13).

Joseph had a dream that it would be right to marry Mary because her pregnancy was by the Holy Spirit (v. 20). It was in a dream that he was warned to flee from Bethlehem and hide Mary and the baby in Egypt because of Herod's murderous jealousy (Matthew 2:13). He knew it was safe to return to Israel with his family, by means of a dream (Matthew 2:19). And another warning came not to settle in Judea but rather in Galilee, Nazareth, through a dream (Matthew 2:22). Three out of the four dreams included an angel communicating to Joseph.

We don't have much information about Joseph in the New Testament Scriptures but of the references we have, many refer to his repeated experiences of divine communication by means of dreams. Did God choose to communicate with him in this way because Joseph was a visual learner? Because he needed vivid persuasion? Whatever the reasons for the dreams and the angels, Joseph paid attention, recognised their source and heeded their message.

Mary too had her own heavenly vision – an encounter with the angel Gabriel, who delivered the message of the ages to her young heart, a message that took root not only in her spirit but in her womb, and gave birth to the Son of God.

Start to finish, this story is surrounded and filled with angels, dreams and visions – Zechariah, father to John the Baptist, was dumbfounded by his angel encounter; the shepherds working the night shift on the hills of Bethlehem were terrified and amazed, first by one angel and then by a sky full of them, singing!

If angels and dreams and visions are the language of heaven to earth, is it any wonder that this story is saturated in such things? Why should we be surprised that God would speak to Mary and to Joseph by these means? And why would he not speak to us in these same ways?

These are still the days of dreams and still the days of visions – enflamed by the Holy Spirit. Will you watch, will you listen, will you pay attention to the dreams he is sending you? Like Joseph, will you recognise their source and heed their message?

Favour Ain't Fair!

'Then Simeon blessed them and said to Mary, his mother: "This child is destined to cause the falling and rising of many in Israel, and to be a sign that will be spoken against, so that the thoughts of many hearts will be revealed. And a sword will pierce your own soul too"' (vv. 34, 35).

'**S**lap someone and say, "Favour ain't fair!"' Thus exhorted Bishop T. D. Jakes, founder and pastor of mega-church The Potter's House, to his listening audience. He offered this as a suggested response to the ecstasy of experiencing the biblical concept of the favour of God. It just isn't fair. Living in the favour of God is sometimes so overwhelming that it can leave you speechless – all you can do is 'slap someone'.

The angel Gabriel personally visited Mary and told her explicitly that she was 'highly favoured' (Luke 1:28). Then, in case she had missed the point, just a moment later he underscored the fact that she had found favour with God. Mary had been chosen to bear the Son of the Most High, who would inherit the throne of King David, and his kingdom would never end!

Then, just a few days after the birth of Jesus, Mary and Joseph bring him to the temple and suddenly another jolting prophecy came from old man Simeon. Mary heard that her son will be spoken against. A sword will pierce her soul? That's not fair. What about all that favour?

The grown-up Jesus – master teacher, rabbi – taught and warned his followers of a similar paradoxical message: there is something about intimate relationship with Jesus that offers the greatest joy, the deepest fulfilment, the most transformational love – living in the favour of God. Intrinsic to this relationship is inexplicable hostility, irrational opposition, heartbreaking rejection and sorrow.

How are you sharing in ever-deepening union with Jesus Christ? In what ways is his favour upon your life? Where do you experience the fellowship of Christ's sufferings?

———————

To ponder:

'If you are insulted because of the name of Christ, you are blessed, for the Spirit of glory and of God rests on you.'

(1 Peter 4:14)

The Family Business

'And he said to them, "Why did you seek me? Did you not know that
I must be about my Father's business?"' (v. 49, NKJV).

Mary and Joseph did so many things right. They were both righteous before God. They were counted trustworthy to bear and raise the Son of God. They were both humble-hearted, both heeded the angelic messages delivered to them, both were willing to surrender their reputations and plans in order to be useful for God's purposes through them. They obeyed the law of the government – the Roman rulers – and so went to Bethlehem for the census. They obeyed the laws of religion – in their case Judaism – and brought Jesus to the temple for dedication at eight days old and offered sacrifices there according to Hebrew Scripture (Luke 2:22, 23). They also went to Jerusalem every year for the feast of the Passover (Luke 2:41, 42).

This one story about Jesus as a child – after his miraculous birth in Bethlehem but before his entrance on the scene of public ministry – recorded for us in the second chapter of the Gospel of Luke, shows us that Mary and Joseph continued in their 'holy habits' with regard to their faith and in raising Jesus in the way of righteousness. They were in the community of believers, observing the customs and obeying the law of Moses. They loved Jesus; they knew he was special, God-sent.

Yet the twelve-year-old Jesus succeeded in stretching their understanding of what his life was about. It was about doing his 'Father's business'. But even in the stretching, Jesus was submissive to them. Mary and Joseph and Jesus demonstrate a loving, yielding, submitting, stretching, dynamic relationship with one another as fellow-pilgrims.

How about you? What are some ways in which you have settled down in your faith understanding, feeling familiar with Jesus, acquainted with the laws, customs, expectations, and perhaps irritated when that is upset? Ask Jesus to stretch you beyond what you think you know to something more. Ask him to grant you a larger perspective of what it means in your life to allow Jesus to be about his Father's business – in you.

Thanks to God

As the northern hemisphere begins spring and the southern starts autumn, and as some countries celebrate Mothering Sunday, from full hearts we all lift our thanks to God – the Giver of all good.

Now thank we all our God
With hearts and hands and voices,
Who wondrous things hath done,
In whom his world rejoices;
Who from our mother's arms
Hath blessed on our way
With countless gifts of love,
And still is ours today.

O may this bounteous God
Through all our life be near us,
With ever-joyful hearts
And blessèd peace to cheer us,
And keep us in his grace,
And guide us when perplexed,
And free us from all ills
In this world and the next.

All praise and thanks to God
The Father now be given,
The Son and him who reigns
With them in highest Heaven.
The one eternal God,
Whom earth and Heaven adore;
For thus it was, is now,
And shall be evermore.

Martin Rinkart,
trs. Catherine Winkworth

(4) Priscilla and Aquila
Quite the Couple!

'Greet Priscilla and Aquila, my fellow-workers in Christ Jesus'
(Romans 16:3).

Priscilla and Aquila stand as an exemplary egalitarian couple. Their enlightened ministry provides a perfect model for ministry. Several distinguishing principles emerge. They come from different backgrounds – Aquila is a Jew from Pontus and Priscilla is a Gentile – and yet they are clearly *together* in ministry. They are always mentioned as a couple – there is no reference to either one individually – and in four of their six biblical references Priscilla is mentioned first.

This literary structure communicates much about their force as a couple, and their own relationship. 'The fact that Priscilla's name is mentioned several times before that of her husband has called forth a number of conjectures. The best explanation seems to be that she was the stronger character,' comments the *International Standard Bible Encyclopedia.*

Ethnic – and perhaps temperamental – differences notwithstanding, their marriage simply had to be strong to endure the recorded stresses they faced. Could it be that a subtle and sanctified principle is inserted into the New Testament? Today's sociologists might agree – the record shows that the family in which one person makes all decisions is not the healthiest. Indeed, one study notes that a strong indicator of impending divorce is a husband's refusal to listen to his wife. The lowest rates of abuse and dysfunction are found in families where decisions are made democratically.

Social scientists have also noticed that across a variety of cultures, the most satisfying marriages are where either the couple negotiates all decisions jointly or they have separate areas of responsibility.

Wow! Well done, Priscilla and Aquila – or should we say, Aquila and Priscilla? Either way there is a lesson for us: do I listen, or do I habitually insert my clever ideas into the 'conversation'? Am I mature enough to absorb 'second billing' without rancour? Who are the couples you know who equate with Priscilla and Aquila? Thank God for them today.

Two verses from magnificent Romans 12 seem to apply here: 'Do not think of yourself more highly than you ought' (v. 3) and 'Honour one another above yourselves' (v. 10).

Background Influence

'Though one may be overpowered, two can defend themselves.
A cord of three strands is not quickly broken' (Ecclesiastes 4:12).

A church leadership book causing some buzz these days is *Leading from the Second Chair* by Mike Bonem and Roger Patterson. One reviewer succinctly observes: 'This book cautions second chair leaders to check their personal egos at the door when they enter.' Truth be told, most of us serve in secondary roles, but the potential for genuine and lasting contribution should never be underestimated. Our couple of the week exemplifies this.

Priscilla and Aquila are in the background of the central drama that is the New Testament Church, yet their influence on two larger-than-life characters – Paul and Apollos – is enormous. Talk about first chair leaders!

They work closely with the apostle Paul and their influence is such that when he relocates from Corinth to Ephesus he brings them with him. It is during this time that they invest in the brilliant yet flawed Apollos, and help him come to a more mature understanding of the gospel. Both men are the charismatic headliners, and yet the couple's undemonstrative, steady kindness to Paul and solid teaching with Apollos are simply irreplaceable. One gets the impression that Aquila and Priscilla had 'checked their egos at the door' a long time before.

Priscilla and Aquila are vocational partners and also partners in spirit. It is the force of their contribution *as a couple* that gives such added dimension to their grace. One writer even goes so far as to suggest they 'represent the best of the early Church'. If so, some background influence! Some second chair!

Who are the background couples who have influenced you in your missionary journeys? Unpretentious steadiness often stands the test of time.

————————

To ponder:

Thank God for these unsung heroes. Name them. Bless them. Become them.

Home – A Place of Mission

'Aquila and Priscilla greet you warmly in the Lord, and so does the church that meets at their house' (1 Corinthians 16:19).

Bramwell Booth, The Salvation Army's second General, writes of home visitation with an elderly man he calls 'Old Cornish'. He recalls that these humble meals with a simple man were communion in the deepest sense. Here with this converted drunkard, eating sacramental fried bacon and potatoes and drinking tea, Bramwell remembers that when they knelt down to pray, Old Cornish was so uplifted it seemed he was another man.

Bramwell Booth writes:

> There came to me, in answer to those prayers . . . a new feeling of relationship to the souls of people, a directional impulse, impelling me to love and suffer for the sake of others. Again and again I have come down those old squeaking stairs feeling as though I walked on the wind, and have gone out to Mile End Waste to speak and pray with sinners in altogether a new and self-forgetting fashion.

I am moved at the story not only by the sacramental force and irreplaceable value of pastoral visitation exemplified by Bramwell Booth but also, and equally, by the missional hospitality of Old Cornish. I instantly recall the prayer warriors I have visited, ostensibly to encourage and bless, who have turned the tables on me and summarily seen me depart 'walking on the wind'.

Priscilla and Aquila equally instinctively opened their home for missional purposes. The reference above is one of several that highlight their lifestyle of hospitality. Here they are leading a church in their home in Ephesus; back in Rome, they again host a church in their house: 'Greet Priscilla and Aquila . . . Not only I but all the churches of the Gentiles are grateful to them. Greet also the church that meets at their house' (Romans 16:3–5). Wherever they go, it seems, their home becomes a centre for ministry – 'all the churches of the Gentiles are grateful to them'.

Today, pray over your home. Extend hospitality to someone in need. Get ready to walk on the wind.

A Collaborative Couple

*'Because he was a tentmaker as they were, he stayed and
worked with them' (Acts 18:3).*

In 1990, Alvin Toffler predicted a change in the business climate of the West: 'We can expect to see couples hired by companies – as couples. Before long we will no doubt see a wife-husband team placed in charge of a profit centre and permitted – in fact, encouraged – to run it like a family business.' Nowadays, medical, educational and corporate worlds are discovering that a husband–wife team can be a productive force – and enjoy their marriage while working together.

Priscilla and Aquila are a working couple – tent-making – who also have a sense of mission. Their occupation does not weaken their devotion to each other or their commitment to Christian mission. It is seamlessly fused together. Paul seemed to love it.

A recent commercial development along these lines includes a growing number of 'collaborative couples'. These are couples who head small businesses or entrepreneurships *together*. They are listed as one of the 'megatrends' of the new century.

The healthy couples compete with other businesses, not with each other. They demonstrate both close communication and complementary talents. They function with mutual respect, support each other and maintain balance by keeping the marriage as the predominant relationship. They naturally bring trust, freedom and shared objectives.

This does not mean relinquishing personal identity; rather it means lifetime partners experiencing synergy from each other. These couples experience bonding from working together. They like being together for long periods of time. All this rather sounds like a vitalised, Christian marriage. Is it too fanciful to assert that God's natural design is for men and women to enjoy working together?

All my work is for the Master,
He is all my heart's desire;
O that he may count me faithful
In the day that tries by fire!
Albert Orsborn (SASB 522)

Relocating for Mission

'Paul stayed on in Corinth for some time. Then he left the brothers and sailed for Syria, accompanied by Priscilla and Aquila' (Acts 18:18).

Janet and I once had the pleasure of sitting next to a Benedictine educator during a Salvation Army Christmas luncheon. In the course of easy conversation we discovered he was commencing his fortieth year at the same Roman Catholic college. He had no inkling of moving, having decades earlier taken a Benedictine 'vow of stability'. You can imagine the animated dialogue that immediately followed, as we compared our Salvationist 'vow of itinerancy'! Both are beautiful covenants.

Priscilla and Aquila identify more with Salvationism; they are a working couple who have a sense of mission that entails relocation for the gospel. In terms of how they live their lives and how they view their ministry, they are a wonderful model of flexibility. Their marriage and ministry means regular travel in what was then a very dangerous world. Yet – here is the paradox – their home was evidently still a wonderfully attractive place of worship, hospitality and refuge. Aquila and Priscilla travel, yet the road doesn't seem to 'own them'.

There is risk to the gospel, and exercising faith often means a journey into the unknown. This can be disconcerting. That which is unfamiliar to us is unsettling by definition. Jesus says: 'Everyone who has left houses or brothers or sisters or father or mother or children or fields for my sake will receive a hundred times as much and will inherit eternal life' (Matthew 19:29).

We all need home; however, it does seem that God has a special blessing for those who leave secure surroundings for the cause of the gospel. These sojourners will inherit an everlasting room prepared for them. One day they will finally come home.

To pray:

Lord Jesus, if staying home means that I am compromising faith, please evict me. I am comforted that you know what it means to leave home. You also promised me a place in your Father's house. Can you make sure I'm close to the family I left behind?

Impact Together

' "*You know that the rulers of the Gentiles lord it over them, and their high officials exercise authority over them. Not so with you. Instead, whoever wants to become great among you must be your servant*" ' (Matthew 20:25, 26).

The marriage of William and Catherine Booth helped chart the course for The Salvation Army. Their union is one of the great Victorian romances. They were devoted to each other from the beginning. Their biographer Roy Hattersley writes:

> They shared the same failings and foibles and lived for 40 years in something close to complete harmony. The extraordinary quality of their relationship was the way in which characteristics which might have driven them apart served only to bind them more closely together.[9]

Catherine bore eight children and yet always remained at the forefront of ministry and the co-founding of a movement. And remember, this was during times of acute persecution.

In an age when the focus is mostly on what happens between husband and wife, William and Catherine Booth – like Aquila and Priscilla – are an example of what can happen *through* husband and wife. Their effectiveness together speaks about their relationship with each other.

The words of the Early Church father Tertullian, extolling the beauty of marriage, can be readily applied to couples in mission:

> How beautiful, then, the marriage of two Christians, two who are one in hope, one in desire, one by the way of life they follow, one in the religion they practise.
>
> They are as brother and sister, both servants of the same Master.
>
> Nothing divides them, either in flesh or in spirit.
>
> They are, in very truth, two in one flesh; and where there is but one flesh there is also but one spirit.
>
> They pray together; they worship together; they fast together; instructing one another, encouraging one another, strengthening one another.
>
> Side by side they visit God's Church and partake of God's banquet.
>
> Side by side they face difficulties and persecution, share their consolations.
>
> They have no secrets from one another; they never shun each other's company; they never bring sorrow to each other's hearts.
>
> Hearing and seeing this, Christ rejoices.

They suitably conclude the essence of this series – Partnerships in Ministry. We pray them for you, and the marriages in your life.

Pure-hearted

The earth is the LORD's, and everything in it,
the world, and all who live in it;
for he founded it upon the seas
and established it upon the waters.

Who may ascend the hill of the LORD?
Who may stand in his holy place?
He who has clean hands and a pure heart,
who does not lift up his soul to an idol
or swear by what is false.
He will receive blessing from the LORD
and vindication from God his Saviour.
Such is the generation of those who seek him,
who seek your face, O God of Jacob.

Selah

Lift up your heads, O you gates;
be lifted up, you ancient doors,
that the King of glory may come in.
Who is this King of glory?
The LORD strong and mighty,
the LORD mighty in battle.
Lift up your heads, O you gates;
lift them up, you ancient doors,
that the King of glory may come in.
Who is he, this King of glory?
The LORD Almighty –
he is the King of glory.

Selah

Who are the clean-handed and pure-hearted of verse 4? Those redeemed and cleansed through faith in Christ as Saviour. By his grace we join in worshipping him today.

In Galilee

Matthew, a disciple of Christ, wrote his Gospel for the Jews. It seems fitting that it comes first in the New Testament as a bridge between the Old and New. Matthew presents Jesus as the fulfilment of the Old Testament, the Messiah. The genealogy of Jesus, placed at the opening of the book establishes Jesus' ancestry with readers. It starts at Abraham and also shows that Jesus is an heir of David.

The Gospel of Mark, written earlier, may have provided the basis for the Gospel of Matthew since most of the material in Matthew is also found in Mark. In Matthew's account Jesus frequently refers to the Old Testament with 'it is written' but sometimes he says 'it was said' and points out that certain men had burdened people through oral law with layers of legalism that were never intended.

Matthew does not explain Jewish customs as some of the other Gospel writers do, which implies he doesn't need to. He refers more to the law of Moses and gives more Old Testament prophecy fulfilments than the other writers do. Matthew emphasises 'righteousness' and the 'kingdom'. He presents Jesus as King as well as Messiah. He ends his record with the resurrection and great commission.

Matthew is said to present his material in a systematic order – possibly reflecting his business training as a tax collector. Compared with the other Gospels his narrative is more of an overview of several categories: Jesus' teachings, his activities and their outcomes.

We will begin in chapter 5 just after the Beatitudes and continue through to chapter 10 when Jesus sends out his twelve disciples on their first mission trip. These chapters are set in the region of Galilee in northern Israel.

Part-way into the study we of course relive Holy Week, as recorded for us by Matthew in chapters 21 to 28.

> In simple trust like theirs who heard,
> Beside the Syrian sea,
> The gracious calling of the Lord,
> Let us, like them, without a word
> Rise up and follow thee.
> *John Greenleaf Whittier*

Saline Solution

' *"Let me tell you why you are here. You're here to be salt-seasoning*
that brings out the God-flavours of this earth" ' *(v. 13*, MSG*)*.

In February we noted that the Epistle of James reflected some of Jesus' Sermon on the Mount. In Matthew 5–7, Jesus is seated on the mountainside, probably overlooking the Sea of Galilee. His disciples are nearest to him, but others can hear him as well. After the well-known Beatitudes he continues with details about how a person with the fresh character he prescribes makes an impact on the world. He begins with a metaphor of ordinary salt.

In addition to its household uses, salt was part of temple sacrifices and symbolic of covenants. Simple salt is so plentiful that we sometimes take it for granted, yet in proper balance it is essential to our health. At times people need it intravenously. Besides being valued for its seasoning, preserving, cleansing and healing properties, in various cultures salt has been used in gestures of hospitality and congratulations. For thousands of years salt was a prized commodity that was sometimes heavily taxed. India remembers Gandhi's symbolic walk to the sea to gather tax-free salt for the nation's poor.

Followers of Christ are to have qualities of salt: a purifying influence, one that enhances and balances life as well as one that makes those we meet thirst for God. As the title of Rebecca Manley Pippert's bestselling book states, Christians should be *Out of the Salt Shaker and into the World*.

Jesus warned against losing our saltiness. The Jordan River flows south from Galilee into the Dead, or Salt, Sea – abundant in the mineral. There was a type of salt there that easily lost its sodium chloride content and became tasteless. It was used to prevent slipping in wet weather as we might use rock salt on icy pavements. Perhaps that was what Jesus had in mind when he said that bland salt wasn't good for anything more than being trampled under foot.

Light

*' "In the same way, let your light shine before men, that they may
see your good deeds and praise your Father in heaven" ' (v. 16).*

After Jesus says that believers are salt, he calls us light (v. 14). Have you heard
of salt lamps? They are made from salt crystals and, when lit, are said to give
off healthful negative ions to purify the air. Jesus spoke about his followers being
both salt and light; perhaps we're the original salt lamps.

As a child, the first Bible verse I memorised was our key verse today. James the
Just would endorse the way it tells us to let what we do reveal what we believe so
that anyone watching will be pointed to God. In a recurring childhood dream I
descended into a dark cavernous space, groped along a tunnel, drawn to light
pouring out of an open doorway. When I got to the threshold of the light-flooded
room I saw Jesus and was safe. The light came from him.

The light which first shone from the life of Jesus was given to a relatively few
men and women who guarded and treasured it. They enfolded it with their lives
to keep it from being blown out. But they not only guarded the light, they lit the
lamps of their lives in its flame. People went with those lighted lives all over the
world.

The light of Christian living still burns – sometimes faintly, sometimes
intensely. The Church keeps the flame of the life of Christ alight in order that
others may light the lamps of their lives at its flame and walk in the way of God
without falling.

> Make me
> a still place of light,
> a still place of love
> of you,
> your light radiating,
> your love vibrating,
> your touch and your healing
> far flung and near
> to the myriads caught
> in darkness, in sickness,
> in lostness, in fear.
> Make a heart-centre here,
> Light of the World.
> *Anonymous*

On the Contrary

'"Be perfect, therefore, as your heavenly Father is perfect"' (v. 48).

Jesus called his followers salt and light. He expected them to penetrate and permeate their world, to help it and to heal it, without fanfare. Salt and light are silent. Through the rest of chapter 5 and chapters 6 and 7 (the balance of the Sermon on the Mount) Jesus spends time reversing some misconceptions. He astounds the crowds with radical views and instructions.

People wondered if he came to up-end the law, but he said he came to fulfil it. People thought that murder would bring heavy punishment, but he said that even being angry, harbouring malice or insulting someone deserved punishment. People knew that adultery was wrong, but he said that looking at someone with lustful desire was adultery of the heart. People thought that divorce was routine, but he said that divorce was not inevitable and on the wrong grounds was tantamount to adultery. People thought that taking oaths gave weight to their promises, but he said we should just say yes or no without equivocation and mean it. (Does this remind us of something James echoes in his Epistle?)

People thought that paying back injury in kind was just, but Jesus said we should surprise offenders with kindness. People said love your neighbour and hate your enemy, but he said love your enemies and, what is more, pray for them, thereby exhibiting a family resemblance to the heavenly Father who gives sun and rain indiscriminately to the upright and the corrupt. Loving those who love you or speaking only to those who speak to you is no better behaviour than that of those who don't know God.

Jesus said we must be perfect (complete in love) as God is. Is that our heart's aim? Songwriters John Bruce and Ralph Johnson describe such a desire coupled with God's gracious enabling:

> I'll follow thee, the good and the true,
> Keeping the Cross always in view;
> Not losing sight of thy divine love
> Which leads me on to things above.
> Daily receiving
> More of thy grace, Lord;
> Till I am summoned
> To see thy face, Lord;
> Following thee is true holiness,
> Thus, through my life, others I'll bless.[10]

First Things First

' *"But seek first his kingdom and his righteousness, and all these things will be given to you as well"* ' (v. 33).

Jesus continues his Sermon on the Mount with additional radical advice: be careful not to do good deeds publicly to be seen by people. Giving to charity? No announcement please. If you seek applause here, then you've had your reward already. No further heavenly reward will be coming. So decide where you want your reward.

Praying? Take care. Remember who counts – God. Stick to basics, be honest and don't get wordy in prayer. Adding fasting? No dour faces please, that's just a backdoor way of seeking others' approval and cancels heavenly rewards. God knows what you do and why. Let it be your secret with God. He'll suit the reward to the deed and motive.

Don't strive to accumulate treasure here. Heavenly treasure is long-lasting and in the end you will want to be where your treasure is. Keep a single mind and single master unless you want to live a fretful, purposeless life. Stop being perpetually worried. Don't you have a heavenly Father? Look at the birds. He takes care of them and you are worth more than they are. God knows your needs.

Seek first things first – God's kingdom and righteousness. Through your faith in Christ, God credits you with his righteousness and imparts righteousness to your heart. God will take care of your tomorrows, so don't worry about them. One day at a time. Or as *The Message* puts it:

Steep your life in God-reality, God-initiative, God-provisions. Don't worry about missing out. You'll find all your everyday human concerns will be met. Give your entire attention to what God is doing right now, and don't get worked up about what may or may not happen tomorrow. God will help you deal with whatever hard things come up when the time comes. (vv. 33, 34)

Although based on Paul's words to the Philippians (4:6, 7), John Larsson's song is a fit conclusion here:

> The Lord is near; have no anxiety,
> Make your requests known to God in prayer.
> Then the peace of God,
> Which is beyond our understanding,
> Will keep guard o'er your hearts and thoughts.[11]

Teacher of the Ages

'When Jesus had finished saying these things, the crowds were amazed at his teaching' (v. 28).

Jesus continued with his sweeping message on the mountainside in the open air. Be perfect (mature) and whole, as God is. Don't judge or you can expect the same judgment used on you. Keep asking, seeking and knocking in prayer. Want to be treated fairly? Treat others that way. 'Here is a simple, rule-of-thumb guide for behaviour: Ask yourself what you want people to do for you, then grab the initiative and do it for them' (v. 12, *MSG*).

Follow the narrow way. The easiest way isn't necessarily the best way. Watch out for false prophets – you'll know them by what they produce. Don't just say, 'Jesus is Lord' but *do* God's will and *prove* it. Act like someone who is smart enough to know what is solid and true and lives accordingly.

No wonder the crowds were astonished at *what* Jesus taught. They would be enthralled by *the way* he taught too – with originality, creativity and an awareness of their needs. He began with the known. In recent memory Herod had fortified his stronghold of Masada on a rocky plateau above cliffs near the Dead Sea. And all Israel was known for its stony soil and rocky outcrops. It was a perfect setting to talk about the wisdom of building a house on rock. It would be strenuous work but have long-lasting results.

Jesus' hearers would understand his simile. He used everyday illustrations, did not avoid difficult topics and reflected intimate knowledge of Scripture and the divinity. Scripture says they were taken aback by *how* he taught as well. Unlike the religious leaders, he taught with the authority of one who knew his subject intimately (v. 29). Jesus is the expert.

It's interesting that the words 'authority' and 'author' have similar origins. It could be said more accurately of Jesus (the Word made flesh) than of anyone else, that he wrote the book on humankind's encounter with God.

His hearers would have made Jesus Teacher of the Year. We who know him as Saviour would call him Teacher of the Ages.

To pray:

Thank God for teachers who have made a lasting impact on your life. Pray too for Christian teachers.

At the End of the Day

'This was to fulfil what was spoken through the prophet Isaiah:
"He took up our infirmities and carried our diseases"' (v. 17).

After the teaching chapters of 5, 6 and 7, Matthew records several miracles in chapters 8 and 9. After Jesus taught with authority, he demonstrated his divine authority through miracles. Our passage contains three healing miracles.

The first miracle recorded in Matthew is the cleansing of a leper (vv. 2–4). It is also found in Mark 1 and Luke 5. The unmistakable infectious skin disease was so dreadful that the Jews believed only God could take it away. How appropriate that Matthew, writing for Jews, chose to record it as Jesus' first healing! By touching the man, Jesus would have become ceremonially unclean, but instead his power cleansed the leper! Jesus ordered the man to have the healing confirmed by the priest as the law dictated. A leper's healing implied a Messiah's presence.

Next, Jesus heals the centurion's young servant who is too ill to be brought to Jesus. The officer shows a thoughtful concern for the young man not always seen between master and servant. The centurion has enough trust in Christ's ability and acquaintance with effective delegated authority to ask Jesus just to say the word. Jesus marvels at his faith and commends the man and all non-Jews who would enter the kingdom of God following his example. The boy was healed.

The third healing miracle was at Peter's house. In the description recorded in Mark 1 and Luke 4 the incident takes place when Jesus and his disciples returned from the synagogue on the Sabbath. Peter's mother-in-law was lying down with a fever. Jesus touched her hand and the fever left. She was well enough to minister to them right away.

Three different people had very different physical needs, but Jesus healed them all. We're also told that Jesus healed all the sick brought to him that Saturday evening (v. 16). Characteristically, Matthew says in verse 17 that what Jesus had done that day was a fulfilment of an Old Testament passage about the Messiah (Isaiah 53:4).

To ponder:

At the end of the day, Jesus is our hope.

Do You Hear What I Hear?

' "Do you hear what these children are saying?" they asked him' (v. 16).

Although all four Gospels include the triumphal entry into Jerusalem, Matthew's is the only account that mentions a donkey *and* her colt. Perhaps it was natural for the mother to accompany her foal. We think of a donkey as a humble mode of travel, but the Old Testament tells of important people who rode donkeys. Yet Jesus rode on the donkey's foal, and it's the only occasion recorded of his riding a donkey at all. Riding a donkey rather than a horse indicated a time of peace rather than war. Matthew says Jesus' entry fulfilled the Messianic prophecy of Zechariah 9:9. Jesus' aspect was Prince of Peace rather than captain of a conquering army that day.

What do we hear? What are the people chanting about the Master now? Verse 9 tells that from all sides Jesus hears Scripture. The words came from one of the six songs of the *Hallel* (Psalms 113–118). The *Hallel* was often used as a unit on joyous occasions. 'Hosanna' meant 'Save us, we pray' and could convey notes of both praise and petition. In the Gospel account we hear a couple of the *Hallel*'s verses: Psalm 118:25, 26. Even the children join in and shout hosannas. The excerpt the people repeated was more relevant than anyone but Jesus would have known as he entered the Holy City.

A large animated crowd moves slowly, steadily into Jerusalem. Some of the pilgrims coming for Passover lay down items of clothing, others cut branches, carpeting the way for Jesus. A new Salvation Army corps (church) was started in a small community in New England, USA. The limited space accommodated a full complement of meetings, programmes, social outreach and office activity. The long-awaited carpet for the single meeting room's concrete floor finally arrived the first week of April. The first meetings in the carpeted room were on Palm Sunday. No noise of chairs scraping the floor or children's dropped coins clattering now. In a curious way, the new carpet was a path for the Lord. The songs of praise resonated differently, yet joyously that Sunday.

What do those around us hear as we worship Christ, our coming King, on this Palm Sunday?

From the Fig Tree

' "Now learn this lesson from the fig-tree: As soon as its twigs get tender and its leaves come out, you know that summer is near" ' (Matthew 24:32).

After the excitement of the triumphal entry and the commotion of cleansing the temple, the disciples and Jesus spent Sunday evening in relatively quiet Bethany. Early the next morning they went back to the city. Jesus saw a fig tree and approached it expectantly. He was hungry. Fruit begins to form on some fig trees as soon as leaves appear. If it didn't have fruit it shouldn't have had leaves either. Interestingly, the name of the town where the disciples had procured a donkey the day before was Bethphage, meaning 'house of figs'. The area was known for its figs.

Figs were part of Jewish history. When prophets spoke about a prosperous, peaceful time, they said that everyone would sit under his own fig tree. A developed fig tree could give refreshing shade and provide a type of spare outdoor room – for meditation or study. When Nathanael met Jesus and the Master said he had seen him under the fig tree before Philip called him, Nathanael was astonished. He declared him Rabbi, Son of God, King of Israel. Jesus told him he would see greater things than Christ's inexplicable knowledge of him (John 1:43–51).

Using the fig tree illustration now would have arrested Nathanael's attention. When Jesus cursed the tree for its lack of fruit, it withered. Jesus used the event as an object lesson about faith and prayer, and repeated what he said about faith in Matthew 17:20. Jesus also drew on the shrivelled tree to warn against hypocrisy. He cautioned that people who pretend to have fruit but have only leaves may seem religious but are not yielding spiritual produce. The disciples would see such people repeatedly that week as they ran into controversies with the Jewish leaders.

The fig tree can be a sign of the season. In Palestine it shows foliage later than other fruit trees. As its leaves develop and their colour deepens it can mean that summer is coming soon. During Holy Week, Jesus also gave attention to his Second Coming (see Matthew 24) and employed the fig tree metaphor again. 'Now learn this lesson from the fig-tree: As soon as its twigs get tender and its leaves come out, you know that summer is near' (v. 32). He urged alertness to the coming of the Son of Man. Spiritual alertness today as we await his return can bear kingdom fruit in our lives.

No More Questions

*'No-one could say a word in reply, and from that day on no-one
dared to ask him any more questions' (v. 46).*

During Holy Week Jesus and his disciples spent time in Jerusalem. He freely engaged the religious leaders who publicly questioned his authority (Matthew 21:23–27). He interspersed direct dialogue with affecting parables about sons, tenants and weddings. The Pharisees, ever Jesus' opponents, in part because he wouldn't accept their teachings of oral law, began to plot ways to entrap Jesus in his words. They thought they had a clever question about taxes. His reply amazed the questioners and they soon left.

Next, the Sadducees who opposed the oral law and believed only in the first five books of the Old Testament as ultimate authority, came with questions allegedly about marriage, but really about the resurrection. Jesus' reply to them astonished everyone.

Then he encountered the Pharisees again. They exercised control over the public partly because they ran the synagogues. They heard that Jesus had got the better of the Sadducees, so they had an expert in the law ask Jesus which commandment was greatest. Jesus' classic answer from Deuteronomy and Leviticus set them buzzing. Now Jesus turned the tables with his own question, which confounded and dumbfounded them. That was the end of the questions.

Even though Matthew's record often telescopes multiple events into one, even his report includes numerous encounters, teachings and parables during this last week of Jesus before the crucifixion. We can assume there were even more. What a full week!

Perhaps it isn't surprising that the religious leaders visited the high priest and plotted to arrest Jesus in some shrewd way and then kill him. Judas would give them opportunity. One party believed in angels and demons, the other didn't. One believed in reaching God by obeying the law; the other didn't believe God cared what people did. One embraced the whole Old Testament plus oral traditions; the other clung to books of Moses alone. One sought converts; the other was elitist and political. It is telling that people who were so different in their points of reference could be so united against Christ.

Do we see coalitions forming against the Lord in our day? Why do people fear truth? How can we present Christ courageously and warmly?

Gathered

' "*O Jerusalem, Jerusalem, you who kill the prophets and stone those sent to you, how often I have longed to gather your children together, as a hen gathers her chicks under her wings, but you were not willing*" ' (v. 37).

After the verbal sparring with religious leaders, Jesus stoutly warned of their folly and counselled his disciples and the crowds not to follow the example of such blind guides. Jesus' ensuing lament over Jerusalem is all the more heartbreaking.

Of the many references to birds generally and specifically, only two references to the hen occur in Scripture – our key verse and Luke's comparable record. Although the Greek word translated 'hen' can refer to any female bird, not just domesticated fowl, what image comes to mind when we read of a hen taking her chicks under her wings? There are purportedly more chickens in the world than any other type of bird and they may even be found in cities. On a drive around a lake in our area we encountered a dozen plump grey speckled hens perched on a garden fence and making unusual sounds. They were guinea fowl.

Psalmists use the metaphor of being under God's wing to indicate protection and safety:

He who dwells in the shelter of the Most High will rest in the shadow of the Almighty. I will say of the LORD, 'He is my refuge and my fortress, my God, in whom I trust.' Surely he will save you from the fowler's snare and from the deadly pestilence. He will cover you with his feathers, and under his wings you will find refuge; his faithfulness will be your shield and rampart. (Psalm 91:1–4)

The concept of a hen gathering her chicks is used figuratively of God's motherly care for his people. It stands, too, as a reminder of Christ's self-sacrifice and tenderness. Although there may be only two references to hens in Scripture, another associated word is used repeatedly. The root of the word 'Almighty' (*Shaddai*) is the word for breasted. God is the breasted-one under whose shadow his own people may dwell and rest safely. During Holy Week, was Jesus recalling Psalm 91 as he lamented both the Jerusalemites' chronic violent refusal of God's message throughout history and now of God himself?

In a similar passage, Luke says Jesus wept over the city. Pause to pray for those who reject Christ. Pray for the peace of Jerusalem. Thank God for his tender care for his children.

With a Song?

*'When they had sung a hymn, they went out to
the Mount of Olives' (v. 30).*

The first time we read of Jesus going to Jerusalem for Passover was when he was twelve and accompanied his parents. As the first-born male he may have considered those spared during the plague of the first-born in Egypt. Now, some twenty years later, he was in Jerusalem for his last Passover. The disciples, who also were accustomed to keeping Passover in Jerusalem, asked where they should prepare that year's observance. The Israelites who lived in the country seem to have been folded into households in Jerusalem for several days each year wherever there was room.

In addition to his teaching via certain Passover elements, Jesus said and prayed many deeply significant things during the Last Supper. The Gospels record some that we can ponder reverently. Various churches conduct Seder services on the Thursday of Holy Week. Understanding some of the Jewish traditions can help inform our understanding. One congregation held an annual Seder on an upper storey, then quietly moved down to a garden setting in the chapel to spend time in prayer with Christ in Gethsemane, as it were.

Scripture tells us the disciples and Jesus sang a hymn before they left for the Mount of Olives. Would we have thought to sing after Jesus had given his last testament? We are told that Psalms 116–118 from the *Hallel* or 'Hallelujah Choruses' of the day (Psalms 113–118) were often used during Passover. The *Hallel* selections were usually sung on joyous occasions. Some *Hallel* verses had been chanted during the triumphal entry on Palm Sunday.

If we knew we were facing death, what would we choose to sing if we sang at all? The final verse of Albert Orsborn's 'My life must be Christ's broken bread' (*SASB* 512) could be our prayer today:

> Lord, let me share that grace of thine
> Wherewith thou didst sustain
> The burden of the fruitful vine,
> The gift of buried grain.
> Who dies with thee, O Word divine,
> Shall rise and live again.

Good Friday

'When the centurion and those with him who were guarding Jesus saw the earthquake and all that had happened, they were terrified, and exclaimed, "Surely he was the Son of God!"' (v. 54).

Prayer for others, especially for those who have wronged us, is the prayer of Good Friday. The prayer of Saturday is the prayer of waiting and release while God works in hidden ways. The prayer of Easter Sunday is one of unexpected life transformation and realised new freedom.

> O love upon a cross impaled,
> My contrite heart is drawn to thee;
> Are thine the hands my pride has nailed,
> And thine the sorrows borne for me?
> Are such the wounds my sin decrees?
> I fall in shame upon my knees.
>
> 'Twere not for sinners such as I
> To gaze upon thy sore distress,
> Or comprehend thy bitter cry
> Of God-forsaken loneliness.
> I shelter from such agonies
> Beneath thy cross, upon my knees.
>
> Forgive! Forgive! I hear thee plead;
> And me forgive! I instant cry.
> For me thy wounds shall intercede,
> For me thy prayer shall make reply;
> I take the grace that flows from these,
> In saving faith, upon my knees.
>
> Now take thy throne, O Crucified,
> And be my love-anointed King!
> The weapons of my sinful pride
> Are broken by thy suffering.
> A captive to love's victories,
> I yield, I yield upon my knees.
> *Albert Orsborn (SASB 122)*

Dark Saturday

*'From noon until three in the afternoon darkness came over
all the land' (Matthew 27:45, TNIV).*

Jesus' night-time struggle in Gethsemane, betrayal, arrest, trial, torture, agonising crucifixion, separation from God and death were all part of the affliction he endured for us, for our salvation. Only love could have motivated such suffering.

Traditionally the daily sacrifice was slaughtered at 3 p.m., including on the day of Passover. At that time a priest stood at the pinnacle of the temple and blew the *shofar* or ram's horn. As Jesus hung on the cross, would he have heard the *shofar* blast and recognised that as the Passover lamb was slaughtered, the hour of his sacrifice as the Lamb of God had come?

We don't know how the three hours of darkness during Jesus' six hours on the cross affected him or the bystanders. Were the disciples recalling deserting Christ, or Peter thinking of his denying Jesus in the darkness the night before? It certainly must have seemed unusual, if not alarming, for there to have been such darkness beginning at midday, especially as other singular events began to happen.

When Luke says that the sun stopped shining, he adds that the temple curtain was torn in two (Luke 23:45). Mark and Matthew link the curtain being torn with the timing of Jesus' last breath. Matthew adds that there was an earthquake, tombs opened and many holy people were raised to life (Matthew 27:51, 52). People may have been accustomed to hearing the *shofar*, but not to experiencing any of the other remarkable events of that day. The literal darkness would have accentuated everything.

Evening was approaching when Jesus' follower, Joseph of Arimathea, asked Pilate for Jesus' body. As he acted out of love at dusk, two Marys sat opposite the tomb, watching in spite of the looming darkness and any misgivings they might have had. They certainly did not anticipate the even more startling events of Easter.

In his book, *Life Together*, Dietrich Bonhoeffer says:

At night Christ was born, a light in the darkness; noonday turned to night when Christ suffered and died on the Cross. But in the dawn of Easter morning, Christ rose in victory from the grave. Morning does not belong to the individual, but to the Church of the triune God, to the Christian family, to the brotherhood of believers.[12]

Easter

'Suddenly Jesus met them. "Greetings," he said. They came to him, clasped his feet and worshipped him. Then Jesus said to them, "Do not be afraid. Go and tell my brothers to go to Galilee; there they will see me"' (vv. 9, 10).

Christian faith, based on the historic facts of Jesus' life and death, becomes the transforming faith of redemption and reconciliation when we encounter the Resurrected Christ.

> No extent of worldly wisdom
> or historical testimony
> can finally establish for us
> the fact and power of Christ's Resurrection,
> unless we have proof in ourselves
> of his Presence
> as a living Spirit . . .
>
> That is the knowledge which
> cleanses the heart,
> destroys the strength of evil
> and brings in that true righteousness
> which is the power to do right.
> That is the greatest proof
> of the Resurrection.
>
> No books, not even the Bible itself;
> no testimony, not even the testimony
> of those who were present
> on that first Easter day,
> can be as good as this,
> the experimental proof.
> It is the most fitting and grateful,
> and adapts itself to every type of human experience.
> And it is beyond contradiction!
> *General Bramwell Booth*[13]

Point of Need

'When he arrived at the other side in the region of the Gadarenes, two demon-possessed men coming from the tombs met him' (v. 28).

In addition to the sick, people also brought the demon-possessed to Jesus and he cast out the evil spirits (v. 16). When Jesus saw the crowd around him he gave orders to cross the lake. He got into the boat and his disciples followed. The well-known account of the life-threatening tempest when Jesus calmed the storm and dumbfounded the disciples demonstrated Jesus' power over nature. It wouldn't be the last miracle of that kind that the disciples would witness.

Next Matthew records that, on the other side, two demon-possessed men came toward Jesus from the tombs. (Mark and Luke also placed this scene after the storm on the sea, but they only mention one man, perhaps the wilder of the two.) Naturally people avoided passing through the area where the violent men lived. We wonder if that meant no one could visit loved ones' graves or that no one could take a public footpath through the area. But Jesus did not avoid the area or the men.

The demons knew who Jesus was and said so. They asked him to send them into the pigs if he planned to drive them out. His 'Go!' of verse 32 was all it took. The demons left, the pigs plunged to their deaths and, although Matthew does not spell it out, we know from the other accounts that the wild men became normal and calm. It was the townspeople who acted unreasonably. They asked Jesus to leave! They missed the greatest opportunity of their lives: to come to know Christ.

When the demoniacs met Jesus they encountered God's mercy at the point of their greatest need. In our own way, today, we may also – for as a fellow Salvation Army officer once said: 'When God wants to bless us he starts with our need.' If we sing, 'Heavenly Father, bless me now', do we mean it? Are we willing for God to touch our lives at the point of our deepest need?

Mark and Luke record that the changed man wanted to go with Jesus. He redirected the man's zeal to telling those at home about what God had done for him.

———

To ponder:

Who is waiting to hear what God has done in my life?

Take Heart!

'Some men brought to him a paralytic, lying on a mat.
When Jesus saw their faith, he said to the paralytic, "Take heart,
son; your sins are forgiven"' (v. 2).

Jesus returned to Capernaum from the other side of the lake. He was possibly at Peter's house again. People had found him there before. In Mark and Luke's versions of the incident, they record that it was so crowded that the men who brought the paralysed man to Jesus had to resort to desperate measures: uncovering part of the roof. If the house had several rooms, what they uncovered may have been the covered portion of the courtyard in the centre of the house where Jesus was teaching and healing.

Mark says there were four friends of the paralysed man. In active faith, they brought him to Jesus at some expense to themselves. The crowd didn't deter them. Their taxed muscles may have reminded them of their venture for days, but they would have had more vivid memories to supersede any discomfort.

Jesus addressed the invalid kindly and with words he would use on several other occasions: 'Take heart', which meant cheer up or take courage. He would say it to the disciples at the Last Supper: 'I have told you these things, so that in me you may have peace. In this world you will have trouble. But take heart! I have overcome the world' (John 16:33). He says it to us.

Then he followed the uplifting words with the unexpected ones of 'your sins are forgiven'. Some religious leaders who were present murmured that Jesus spoke evil. When Jesus asked them about what they thought they had said quietly only to themselves, it must have been disturbing. Jesus knows what we say within ourselves.

But their opposition did not deter Jesus from the man's need and he spoke an unusual word of healing, 'Get up, take your mat and go home.' And he did. The man no longer needed to be carried. He could walk with his friends.

Jesus' divinity had been displayed. The religious leaders were chagrined. The crowd was filled with the awe that had filled the disciples when Jesus stilled the storm. They praised God.

———

To ponder:

Which of my friends will I offer to bring to Jesus in prayer and deed? Take heart!

Followers of Christ

*'As Jesus went on from there, he saw a man named Matthew
sitting at the tax collector's booth. "Follow me," he told him,
and Matthew got up and followed him' (v. 9).*

In Matthew 8:19–22, after Jesus had healed many at Peter's house and before he crossed the lake, a scribe or teacher (probably a Pharisee) told Jesus he would follow him anywhere. Jesus replied that the 'Son of Man' called nowhere in particular home. That may have discouraged the man's zeal. The Lord understood his real intentions.

Another follower piggybacked on the first fellow's declaration, saying he would follow Jesus eventually, but not just yet. He wanted go home and bury his father. He meant he would go home until his father died and he had received his inheritance. No wonder Jesus replied as he did. Following Christ is not at our own convenience. The King commands allegiance at his pleasure. We don't know if either of the two would-be followers ever made good on their plans.

Now we come to another type of follower. He gave up his occupation to follow Jesus, and eventually to write the Gospel we are reading. Jesus met Matthew. Did his name, which means 'reward or gift of the Lord', imply his parents' attitude towards his birth?

Matthew was a tax collector in Capernaum, perhaps a customs agent. He may have been aware of Jesus' ministry in the area. Matthew calls himself a publican whereas Mark and Luke call him Levi. Those writers tell us he opened his own house to the Lord and gave a great feast. They tell us he left all to follow Christ. Matthew humbly doesn't tell us about these things. Further, when Luke lists the apostles' names in pairs (6:15) it's Matthew and Thomas, but when Matthew gives the list (10:3), it's Thomas and Matthew. When Jesus said, 'Follow me', Matthew did.

Other tax collectors and 'sinners' ate with Jesus and the disciples. We can imagine the Pharisees distancing themselves from such riff-raff and objecting to such a guest list. Maybe they were some of the same elevated religious leaders who had broken the murmur meter when Jesus healed and forgave the paralytic earlier in the chapter. Using sickness as a metaphor for sin, Jesus reminded them that the ill need the doctor, not the well. He came for those who know their need of him. Jesus comes to meet us in ways we may least expect.

Two Twelves

'She said to herself, "If I only touch his cloak, I will be healed"' (v. 21).

When Jesus was finishing up with illustrating that his mission wasn't a repair job, but an entirely new cloth, Jairus came asking for help for his sick twelve-year-old daughter. Meanwhile a woman who was quite alive, but deadened by the pain and shame of a twelve-year-long blood disorder, timidly came within reach of Jesus. Had she just heard him talking about cloth? She told herself that if she could just touch the border of Jesus' garment she would be healed/saved (same root word). Special tassels and ribbon were worn on the borders of cloaks as visual aids to remind Jews to obey God's commandments. Was she thinking of any particular commandment when she approached Jesus and reached for the border of his cloak?

Jesus had said, 'Take heart, son' to the paralytic in Matthew 9 and now he says, 'Take heart, daughter' to this unpretentious woman. Hers wasn't a monumental act, but Jesus, who knows our hearts, knew her motive and intention, commended her faith and healed her. She would no longer be considered ceremonially unclean, no longer have to plan her day around her disorder or spend all her money on doctors. No more soiled cloths to wash out and dry surreptitiously. No more exhaustion due to loss of blood. No more hearing well-meaning friends' remedies or rationale for her condition. No more staying away from religious gatherings. No more contaminating anything and anyone she touched. No more explaining her life away.

We wonder if she might have become one of the women who followed Jesus and the disciples and tended to their needs. Was she one of the women at the cross or in the garden observing where his body was laid and coming on the first day of the week with spices? Was she one of the first to learn of the resurrection?

It was the astounding raising of Jairus' twelve-year-old daughter, not the modest healing of the twelve-year blood-beleaguered woman, that spread Jesus' fame throughout the region that day. But the woman who had previously spent all her living on seeking a cure was both healed and commended for her faith in reaching for Jesus. She too knew the joy of new life.

Our Lord notices us, knows us, loves us – however obscure we think we are.

Number Ten

'And when the demon was driven out, the man who had been
mute spoke. The crowd was amazed and said, "Nothing like
this has ever been seen in Israel"' (v. 33).

Today's passage describes the final two of the ten miracles Matthew groups together in chapters 8 and 9. There were many more, so he must have selected these ten for noteworthy highlights he saw in them. Several point to Jesus' remarkable statements or actions and others to remarkable things others said about Jesus.

When Jesus went indoors (probably at Peter's house again) the blind men who had followed him and called out to him for mercy came to him. No doubt there was a reason this took place indoors. Was it to keep the miracle private? Was it for the sake of the blind men? Even dim light would seem bright to the newly sighted. For the first time Jesus asked if his petitioners believed he was able to do it (cure them). Their 'Yes, Lord' acknowledged him and his Lordship.

Jesus touched their eyes and said that according to their faith it would be done. The fact that their sight was restored verified both their faith in him and his power to heal. Jesus warned them not to publicise their healing. But how could men who had groped their way in and now walked out in confidence not spread the word? His miracles of physical healing authenticated his claims, but his mission was fundamentally for people's spiritual healing.

As the no-longer visually challenged left upbeat, another person in need was brought to Jesus. The man who was demon-possessed and could not talk was healed as well. We're not told who brought him. Jesus did not commend his faith or the faith of friends this time. Jesus knew what was needed. We don't read that Jesus said anything, but when the demon was driven out, the man spoke. What do you think his first words would have been?

What were the reactions to these ten miracles? After some, people wanted to follow Jesus. After one, fearful people asked Jesus to leave. After others, people marvelled and glorified God. Now, following the healing of these three men, everyone said they had never seen the likes of it in Israel. Were the Pharisees just defensive, jealous or protecting their religious traditions with their cynical conclusion that Jesus was an accomplice of Satan? How do we respond to miracles of grace in ourselves and in others today?

His Harvest

' "Ask the Lord of the harvest, therefore, to send out
workers into his harvest field" ' (v. 38).

Jesus continued his ministry in the Galilee region. He went to where the people were, he taught in the synagogues, preached the good news of the gospel, healed the sick and diseased. He had compassion on the crowds whose down-trodden and weary state reminded him of shepherdless sheep. They had been maligned rather than helped by religious leaders of the day.

In the middle of such need Jesus told the disciples to ask God for more workers. What did he mean? The disciples would know since sometimes Jews called their rabbis and students 'reapers' and their teaching a harvest. Jesus called God 'the Lord of the harvest' and the people 'his harvest field'. God has a vested interest in all people. Those who are aware of their need for God are a ripe, ready harvest.

That it is God's field, God's harvest and God's appointment can be a relief. What does he ask of us? To pray he would send more workers. But it doesn't end there, does it? At the beginning of chapter 10 Jesus calls twelve disciples together and gives them authority to drive out evil spirits and heal disease. Matthew names them in pairs – perhaps the way they were commissioned. Asking the Lord of the harvest to send out workers involves being willing to be sent ourselves.

It is currently springtime in the northern hemisphere. Although it may be harvest time south of the equator, those in the north don't usually associate harvest with spring. However, there is a type of wheat that is planted in autumn before the snow comes. Seeds of winter wheat lie dormant until spring when their green shoots enliven the farmer's spirit. What an image of hope!

Some Salvation Army training colleges hold their ordination of new officers in the spring. This year the name of the session being commissioned is Witnesses for Christ – a modern picture of hope. Both metaphors of springtime's new life and labourers for the harvest are apt. God bless the labourers he is still appointing to the urgent task!

To ponder:

When have I asked the Lord of the harvest to send reapers into his harvest field?

Creation Sunday

In some parts of the world the Church observes the nearest Sunday to Earth Day (22 April) as Creation Sunday. At this season there are also various designated days that celebrate spring such as Arbour Day and Japan's *Midori no Hi* (Greenery Day). We acknowledge again, with grateful hearts, our Lord's handiwork and join the psalmist to praise the Creator of all.

> The LORD reigns, he is robed in majesty;
> the LORD is robed in majesty
> and is armed with strength.
> The world is firmly established;
> it cannot be moved.
> Your throne was established long ago;
> you are from all eternity.
>
> The seas have lifted up, O LORD,
> the seas have lifted up their voice;
> the seas have lifted up their pounding waves.
> Mightier than the thunder of the great waters,
> mightier than the breakers of the sea –
> the LORD on high is mighty.
>
> Your statutes stand firm;
> holiness adorns your house
> for endless days, O LORD.

What can I do where I live to relish and celebrate God's creation, care for it and participate in making it better for others?

Mission 101

'These twelve Jesus sent out with the following instructions: "Do not go among the Gentiles or enter any town of the Samaritans"' (v. 5).

In chapter 10, Matthew records Jesus' instructions to the twelve disciples when he sent them out, possibly two by two, as his ambassadors. In this list of the twelve Thomas is partnered with Matthew. We may be remembering Thomas today, since it is eight days after Easter. After the first Easter it was the day Thomas saw the resurrected Christ for the first time (John 20:26).

But in Matthew 10 when Thomas and the others were in the early stages of their walk with Jesus, he sent them on a short-term task in preparation for their ongoing work as apostles. We read such basic tips about discipleship as: take care to depend primarily on God (not on your personal resources) and when you declare the good news know that your message will sometimes be accepted and sometimes rejected.

At this juncture, Jesus instructed the twelve to go to Jews. We may wonder why he limited the disciples' mission field. Although Jesus himself mainly addressed Jews with his message, he certainly included others. Possibly Jesus wanted his followers to relate to people most like themselves in their first venture – Jews to Jews. (Similarly, Jesus had already told some people whom he had healed to go home and tell their story there on home turf.)

The people who would hear the disciples would have a basic understanding of such concepts as 'the kingdom of heaven'. Their preaching would be confirmed by miracles. Jesus told them that they shouldn't take elaborate measures for provisions or try to make an impression with extra money, bags, clothes, shoes. Stuff shouldn't be the focus. They should try living by faith for this venture. Has the Lord ever asked you to do that?

Jesus instructed the twelve about where to stay, how to greet the hosts and what to do if they were not welcomed. 'Shake the dust from your feet' sounds strange to us, but for people in Israel, their land and its dust were special. Other lands were polluted. If people visited another country, they stopped at the border to shake off its dust before re-entering Israel. If they rejected the gospel message, the disciples were to bear witness against them as if they were heathens. No doubt they were glad they weren't alone on this mission. Neither are we.

Without Equivocation

' "*I am sending you out like sheep among wolves. Therefore be as shrewd as snakes and as innocent as doves*" ' *(v. 16).*

The disciples' mission impossible would be possible. When Jesus said, 'I am sending you', the *I* was emphatic and it implied his authority. It also tied with his admonition to them to be simultaneously shrewd and innocent. Be wise because of the wolves; be guileless because of who is sending you and whose you are. Timeless advice.

Jesus continued his instruction. Some of it was for the disciples' immediate mission, but contained principles for their ministry in years ahead. Jesus warned that persecution would come and that they would be delivered to councils and scourged in synagogues (Jewish institutions). They'd also be brought before governors and kings (Gentile powers). They weren't to be concerned ahead of time about what to say or to dwell unnecessarily on the potential coming difficulties. The Spirit of God would provide wisdom.

The warning that sometimes the gospel would also split families might not have been the disciples' initial experience. But Christians around the world have faced this trauma on top of other persecution through the centuries. We have read of the courage of martyrs of other generations as well as in our lifetime. Heaven will reveal the innumerable unknown faithful quiet believers victimised for their faith. For example, Shusaku Endo's historical fiction, *Silence*, reveals the dilemma of persecuted hidden Christians in Japan in the 1600s. And what about Christians of today's persecuted Church?

The disciples were given fair warning about rejection. People would hate them, but Jesus gave the promise of ultimate victory (v. 22). Further, Jesus reminded the disciples that if he had been called Beelzebub his followers should anticipate no better treatment than their master received.

Jesus gave this counsel well before his crucifixion. The twelve could not know what lay ahead for Jesus or for them. No doubt it made more sense to them later. We all tend to think forward, but understand backward. Although the trouble or foes we face may come in different guises, since we trust the Lord and his Word for the mission he's given us, we can know that he accompanies us and will provide.

Sparrow Grace

' "*So don't be afraid; you are worth more than many sparrows*" ' (v. 31).

In spite of the persecution Jesus said would come, he told his disciples they should not be afraid. As to their persecution, Judgment Day would set the record straight. To encourage them, Jesus illustrated God's watchful care by reference to the common sparrow.

On this Earth Day, we too reference God's creatures. Our tortoiseshell cat, Mitsu, bagged a bird one morning. She hydroplaned through the house with feathers in her wake, twice losing and regaining her vice-like grip. After the third jaw adjustment, the bird disappeared behind a floor-length curtain. No amount of shaking the gossamer curtain or peering beneath the sofa revealed the trembling victim. Yet an hour later, a mouse-size form scurried past my feet. Gaining a second wind, it flitted to the kitchen table. Why hadn't Shrewd Hunter detected her prey? Could I aid its escape before Mitsu's interest revived? The bedraggled bird tried a few erratic upsweeps. I propped open the kitchen door and shooed the unravelling ball to open air. The neighbour's evergreen became its recovery perch.

I smiled and pondered. It was a sparrow. Today's key verse came to mind. Wearying illness without resolution conspired to drag my spirit down, but God interposed eternal truth through sparrow grace.

Jesus followed up the assurance with another. If the disciples faithfully and fearlessly proclaimed the truth of Christ and remained loyal to him, he would acknowledge them before the Father. But disowning him would bring his renunciation of them as well. Did Peter remember this conversation when he denied knowing Jesus at the fire outside the high priest's palace? We can take comfort from Jesus' restoration of the remorseful Peter after the resurrection. Peter's one-time denial, although grave, was not mortal.

Is our silence or failure to speak up for him a denial of him? We pray for the Spirit's wisdom, discernment and empowerment to know when to speak and to do it.

Swords and Rewards

' "*Do not suppose that I have come to bring peace to the earth.
I did not come to bring peace, but a sword*" ' *(v. 34).*

In today's key verse Jesus gives a strange word about a sword in his instructions to the disciples. It seems almost out of place following the words of encouragement we considered yesterday.

The first time we read of a sword in connection with Jesus is in the temple when he was about forty days old. The devout elderly Simeon, a resident of Jerusalem, had been told by the Holy Spirit that he would live to see the Messiah. He was moved by the Spirit to go into the temple on the very day Joseph brought Jesus and Mary to the temple for dedication and purification ceremonies.

Simeon held Jesus and praised God for fulfilling his promise of allowing him to see the Messiah before he died. Jesus' parents wondered at Simeon's words about Jesus. Then Simeon blessed them and told Mary the child would cause the rise and fall of many in Israel, be spoken against and cause what was in hearts to be revealed. Then came the stunning word: 'And a sword will pierce your own soul too' (Luke 2:35). Was Simeon referring to Mary's pain at the crucifixion? Yes, and possibly to other suffering she experienced as she released Jesus to ministry and rejection.

One Christmastime in Tokyo Major Yukio Maruhata spoke on this incident in the temple. In the middle of the holiday celebration he asked if embracing Christ had caused a sword to pierce our souls too. He explained that we should expect that following Christ who suffered for us would entail our suffering as well. Perhaps the congregation heard his message in the context of the samurai's sword, a symbol of the spirit of ancient Japan. The sword embodied the samurai's code of honour, steely discipline, devotion and skill.

The sword was commonly recognised in Israel from Old Testament times. Besides its literal uses, the sword was a metaphor for war and for divine justice. The New Testament refers to the Word of God as the sword of the Spirit able to penetrate our soul and spirit. Did Jesus have this sense in mind when he, the Living Word, said he came to bring a sword?

Jesus challenged the disciples: 'Whoever finds his life will lose it, and whoever loses his life for my sake will find it' (v. 39). It's a challenge and promise for us as well.

Open Wide the Windows

Introduction

A radio station in Massachusetts, USA, included a weekly *Pause for Thought*-type programme in which local clergy were invited to share brief inspirational thoughts over the air. The first time I went to the station to record my segment I was shown through to a small cupboard-like interior room. The only window was into the studio control room. Ironically, the programme was called *Through Stained-Glass Windows*.

Do windows intrigue you as they do me? A usual residence in Bible times had few windows. Any facing the road would have been high up, giving good vantage points for observation without allowing access by thieves. The young man Eutychus fell from a third-storey window, where he had been sitting until he dozed off during one of Paul's meetings (Acts 20:9). Some windows had latticework screens. Some had shutters for night-time safety, especially if the buildings were near city walls.

Early windows were chiefly designed to let in light. That was probably the case in the temple King Solomon built (1 Kings 6, 7) as well as in the millennial temple in Ezekiel's vision (Ezekiel 41).

For a few days we will consider literal and figurative windows. As we do, let's pray with Christina Rossetti: 'Open wide the window of our spirits and fill us full of light; open wide the door of our hearts, that we may receive and entertain thee with all our powers of adoration and love.'

Through the Window

*'So she let them down by a rope through the window, for the house
she lived in was part of the city wall' (v. 15).*

At the start of the year, in our Genesis series, we mentioned windows when commenting on the ark Noah built (29 January and 3 February). Commentators believe there was a gap under the roof around the top of the ark. That would have been practical for ventilation and light and would have functioned as a fanlight or window of sorts. Additionally, there was the window Noah was instructed to include and from which he sent the test raven and dove after the deluge ended (Genesis 8:6).

Some translations refer to the beginning of the forty days of torrential rain as the opening of the windows of heaven. In the 1700s, before household drains, people in Britain gave a warning cry – 'gardyloo' – before throwing water out of upper windows. It came from the French, *garde de l'eau* – 'beware the water'. Noah's family could have done with such a warning!

These are the first biblical references to windows. There are a number of others. The picture of the windows of heaven is used again in Malachi:

> Bring all the tithes [the whole tenth of your income] into the storehouse, that there may be food in my house, and prove me now by it, says the LORD of hosts, if I will not open the windows of Heaven for you and pour you out a blessing, that there shall not be room enough to receive it. (3:10, *AB*)

Although windows aren't normally meant to be exits, at times windows provided a welcome way of escape, first for Joshua's spies scouting out Jericho (Joshua 2), then for David fleeing King Saul's wrath (1 Samuel 19:12) and later for Paul escaping danger in Damascus (2 Corinthians 11:33). God made a way!

Open Casements

*'Now when Daniel learned that the decree had been published, he went
home to his upstairs room where the windows opened toward Jerusalem.
Three times a day he got down on his knees and prayed, giving
thanks to his God, just as he had done before' (v. 10).*

Yesterday we mentioned windows used as escapes. In Babylon, Daniel used his
windows differently. He prayed daily from his upper room where his windows
opened toward Jerusalem. Others who have lived far from their homelands might
understand the desire to look homeward, however distant. In the case of exiled
Jews, there was also a pull toward their spiritual north, the temple. It represented
God's presence.

When Daniel learned of a plot against him, which included the decree against
praying to anyone but the king, he went to his regular place of prayer and gave
thanks to God (vv. 10, 11). Regular habits can give us a framework when change
or trouble threatens to confound us – even if we don't face lions every day!

Thanking God is one prayer window. Petition for ourselves and others is
another. Some people keep a prayer journal noting both requests and answers to
prayer. Others keep prayer lists of people and situations. Some join others in
praying for prescribed topics. Church leaders suggest special emphases. There are
special days of prayer on the calendar. We can use missives we receive – from
emails to Christmas cards – to prompt us to pray for the senders. In Japan,
Salvation Army officer-cadets have been taught the practice of praying for the
General at noon every day.

There are times when our chosen patterns need to be refreshed. What prompts
you to this open window? Ultimately, the Holy Spirit who will help us to see
endless creative choices will intercede for us according to God's will (Romans
8:26, 27).

As in this place our hearts are made
To bless thee for thy mighty aid,
Help us, as more for thee we dare,
To prove still more the strength of prayer.
Thy word is sure, thou canst not fail
To bless those who in prayer prevail.
Leslie Rusher (SASB 642)

His Cross

I bring my heart to Jesus, with its fears,
With its hopes and feelings, and its tears;
Him it seeks, and finding, it is blest;
Him it loves, and loving, is at rest.
Walking with my Saviour, heart in heart,
None can part.

I bring my life to Jesus, with its care,
And before his footstool leave it there;
Faded are its treasures, poor and dim;
It is not worth living without him.
More than life is Jesus, love and peace,
Ne'er to cease.

I bring my sins to Jesus, as I pray
That his blood will wash them all away;
While I seek for favour at his feet,
And with tears his promise still repeat,
He doth tell me plainly; Jesus lives
And forgives.

I bring my all to Jesus; he hath seen
How my soul desireth to be clean.
Nothing from his altar I withhold
When his cross of suffering I behold;
And the fire descending brings to me
Liberty.

Herbert H. Booth

This early-day Salvation Army song, 'I bring my heart to Jesus' (*SASB* 420), was written for the movement's 1886 International Congress. Several decades later the fourth verse, with its original fourth line, 'To his cross of suffering I would leap', spoke to Albert Orsborn.

It was a Sunday; Albert Orsborn was in a nursing home convalescing from an accident. He had been resentful of some changes being made to the South London Division which he commanded. When he heard Herbert Booth's song sung, he wept as his spirit was moved and melted. His submission to the Holy Spirit led to the writing of one of his most popular songs, 'Saviour, if my feet have faltered'.

Openings

'So Jesus said again, I assure you, most solemnly I tell you,
that I Myself am the Door for the sheep' (v. 7, AB).

In John 10, Jesus calls himself the door, or gate, for the sheep. He taught that he alone is the way into the sheepfold. Doors imply action. An open door beckons us to discovery or safety. Jesus never called himself a window. It probably wouldn't have been relevant to his hearers. Yet these smaller apertures have something to say to us.

The windows of Bible times were mostly just recessed openings. Glass-making did not develop for some centuries and windows as we know them were not in use until architectural advances allowed them to withstand the weight of roof and walls.

For centuries, colourful church windows have functioned as art, teaching tools, worship aids and memorials. The USA's Washington National Cathedral depicts William Booth in one of its windows. Stained-glass window panels and sun catchers have become popular home decorations in the USA.

During the renovation of the chapel of Asbury Park Salvation Army Corps (church), New Jersey, USA, the defective coloured-glass windowpanes at the centre of the platform wall were removed. Substitute temporary clear-glass panes were installed. The window was in the shape of a cross. For a time the congregation could see the neighbourhood through the cross, a metaphor for Christian mission.

One of New York's historic locations is an unassuming country church, Union Church of Pocantico Hills. It holds treasures, mostly given in memory of members of the Rockefeller family. One is a rose window designed by Henri Matisse. The others represent Old and New Testament figures. They were designed by expatriate Russian Jew Marc Chagall, an artist who explored many artistic methods.

Unlike the composite picture within leaded bounds such as in large Gothic windows of medieval cathedrals, Chagall's stained glass allows figures to flow across panes in a mystical, modern style. The images portray a type of spiritual quality that also suffuses his windows of the twelve tribes of Israel in the synagogue of the Hadassah Hebrew University Medical Centre in Jerusalem. As long as there is light, they're beautiful.

To ponder:

Does God's light shine through me?

Views

*'Your eyes will see the king in his beauty and view
a land that stretches afar' (v. 17).*

Unlike shop windows, windows of homes function mainly to let us look out. Sometimes a view is a corrective to the littleness around us. Yet we cover many of our homes' windows. At times it's for privacy or to filter or block light or heat. In places where sunshine is precious, there are laws governing the height of new buildings to allow for enough sunshine for existing residents in surrounding buildings. Window coverings vary from bamboo screens to lined velvet draperies and include blinds, wooden shutters, exterior German *rolladen,* Japanese *amado* and Bermuda shutters.

In one of Elizabeth Goudge's books, the main character felt that after a day's work he should spend his evening in a room that had windows with lower panes curtained to his everyday world and upper panes open to the far-off horizon, so his commonplace cares could be temporarily forgotten while thoughts of loftier things could be boundless.

Similarly, Salvation Army officers Carl and Gudrun Lydholm wrote about the way their windows and outlooks changed when they moved from a farmhouse to an apartment when their appointment changed from pastoral duties to administrative ones. Literally and figuratively they went from a detailed grassroots outlook and work to a far-reaching overview.

The Bible can function as a window on ordinary daily life as well as a corrective to the littleness around us. William Carey was a village cobbler, minister and schoolmaster. He kept his handmade leather world map on view at home. Following his May 1792 sermon, 'Expect great things from God, attempt great things for God', centred on Isaiah 54:2, 3, Carey and a few others started a missionary society. Carey offered himself as its first missionary, arriving in Calcutta, India, in autumn 1793.

A verse which sums up the life of the man who has been called the father of modern missions is also from Isaiah. It's a key verse today. In the Bible Carey saw the King and on the map, the far horizon. If we truly see both the King in his beauty and the world for which Christ died, won't we want to share him with that world?

Eyethyrls

' "*The eye is the lamp of the body. If your eyes are good, your whole body will be full of light*" ' *(v. 22).*

Clear windows are for seeing through, for keeping an eye on things. Some tall, narrow Dutch houses cleverly combine windows with angled mirrors so anyone on an upper storey can see who is at the door without going down numerous steps. Millions have visited the popular London Eye observation wheel which, as it rotates, raises passengers in huge glass capsules which give extraordinary views of the city below.

Historically, the English language has used some interesting words for windows. *Fenestre*, derived from French and Latin, was used for glazed windows. Colourful *eyethyrl*, an old English word meaning 'eyehole', was also used, but *vind auga* from the Norse (meaning 'wind's eye') became 'window' and finally won out.

Windows have been considered luxuries at times. In England in the 1700s a window tax either limited them or caused people to brick them up. Because people were thus taxed for light and ventilation, windows at times have symbolised status or wealth.

They can be seen as symbols of people's sight and insight as well. Matthew and Luke record Jesus' references to the eye as the lamp of the body. Eugene Peterson introduces an interesting variation of Matthew's verses:

> Your eyes are windows into your body. If you open your eyes wide in wonder and belief, your body fills up with light. If you live squinty-eyed in greed and distrust, your body is a dank cellar. If you pull the blinds on your windows, what a dark life you will have. (Matthew 6:22, 23, *MSG*)

I once hired a window cleaner who cleaned the insides of my windows and promised to return on a warmer day to finish the outsides. In the interim we hung clean curtains at the dust-free interiors, but looked out on a clouded view of the garden. It reminded us of Paul's words: 'For we see now through a dim window obscurely, but then face to face; now I know partially, but then I shall know according as I also have been known' (1 Corinthians 13:12, *DT*). Are we hoping to see clearly through our windows into God's Word? Periodically we need to ask him to remove the film that hinders our view of his truth.

Two-way Windows

'And we all with unveiled face, beholding as in a glass the glory
of the Lord, are transformed into the same image, from glory to glory,
as by the Spirit of the Lord' (v. 18, WNT).

Some say words are windows to our hearts. That could sound one-way, suggestive of cars slowing down to take in shop-window displays. From time to time one-way windows are used to observe people without their knowledge. Sometimes the exterior of an office building with such windows gives a mirror-like reflection of its surroundings – quite different from The Salvation Army's International Headquarters with its transparent aspect. Another one-way window is the media – radio, TV, newspapers, films and websites. Although at their best these can be windows on our world, revealing its needs, they are not substitutes for interacting with reality at first hand. Video-conferences, blogs and mobile-phone video calls can be two-way windows.

From a spiritual perspective, Henri Nouwen in his *Making All Things New* says: 'In true community we are windows constantly offering each other new views on the mystery of God's presence in our lives.'[14]

Doesn't the Bible function that way even more? It's a divine book of many two-way windows set in casements and sashes of 66 books. We read the Word and gain insight into God's nature and will, especially as we consider Christ. And if we invite the Holy Spirit to help us, we may see ourselves from God's point of view and seek his help to obey him. The two verses prior to our key verse indicate a freedom in using this two-way spiritual window: 'But whenever anyone turns to the Lord, the veil is taken away. Now the Lord is the Spirit, and where the Spirit of the Lord is, there is freedom' (2 Corinthians 3:16, 17). Then the key verse gives us the amazing hope of seeing God's glory and being transformed into his glorious image by his Spirit.

———————

To ponder:

When I read the Bible, am I allowing the Bible to read me?

Notes

1. Adam Clarke, *Commentary on The Old Testament* (Abingdon-Cokesbury Press, 1940)
2. Henry Blackaby, *Experiencing God* (Broadman & Holman, 1994)
3. John Gowans, 'His Provision' (Salvationist Publishing and Supplies Ltd, administered by CopyCare, PO Box 77, Hailsham, BN27 3EF, 1985)
4. John Coutts, 'How fearsome and far' (R. G. Publishing)
5. William Booth, *Purity of Heart* (The General of The Salvation Army, 1902, revised edition 2007)
6. Alvin Toffler, *Power Shift* (Bantam, 1990)
7. Ellen White, *Patriarchs and Prophets* (Pacific Press Publishing, 2002)
8. Emily and George Walther, 'Celebrating our partnership', *Priscilla Papers*, Vol. 5, No. 4 (1991)
9. Roy Hattersley, *Blood and Fire* (Abacus, 2000)
10. John Bruce and Ralph Johnson, 'Reckon on me', *The Musical Salvationist* (Salvationist Publishing and Supplies Ltd, 1904, 1990)
11. John Larsson, 'The Lord is near', *Happiness and Harmony* (The General of The Salvation Army, 1990)
12. Dietrich Bonhoeffer, *Life Together* (HarperSanFrancisco, 1978)
13. Bramwell Booth, 'The resurrection and sin', *Our Master* (Salvationist Publishing and Supplies Ltd, 1908)
14. Henri J. M. Nouwen, *Making All Things New: An Invitation to the Spiritual Life* (HarperSanFrancisco, 1981)

Index

Index

January–April 2009

(as from September–December 2003)

Genesis	1–12:9	January–April 2009
	25–35	January–April 2005
Joshua		May–August 2005
1 Samuel	1–16	September–December 2005
1 Samuel	8–15	September–December 2004
1 Kings		September–December 2007
1 Kings 16–2 Kings 2		September–December 2003
Esther		January–April 2009
		May–August 2007
Psalms	23	September–December 2004
	27	January–April 2007
	105–116	September–December 2003
	117–119:104	January–April 2004
	119:105–127	May–August 2004
	128–139	September–December 2004
	140–150	January–April 2005
Isaiah	1–35	May–August 2005
	40	September–December 2005
	41–53	January–April 2006
	54–59	May–August 2006
	60–66	September–December 2006
Proverbs		September–December 2008
Jeremiah	1–17	January–April 2004
Daniel		May–August 2007
Hosea		May–August 2007
Joel		May–August 2004
Amos		January–April 2006
Jonah		May–August 2008
Micah		September–December 2004
		September–December 2008
Habakkuk		January–April 2005

Zephaniah		January–April 2007
Haggai		May–August 2006
Malachi		September–December 2006
Matthew	5–10	January–April 2009
Luke	1–2	September–December 2005
	1–4	September–December 2003
	4:14–7	January–April 2004
	7–9	May–August 2004
	9–12	September–December 2004
	13–16	January–April 2005
	17–21	September–December 2005
	22–24	January–April 2006
John	1–7	May–August 2006
	3:16	January–April 2005
	8–14	September–December 2006
	15–21	January–April 2007
Acts	13–17:15	May–August 2004
	17:16–21:16	May–August 2005
	21:17–26	May–August 2006
	27–28	January–April 2007
Romans		January–April 2004
		May–August 2007
1 Corinthians	1–16	January–April 2008
	13	September–December 2005
2 Corinthians	5:17	January–April 2006
Ephesians		September–December 2008
1 Thessalonians		September–December 2005
2 Thessalonians		January–April 2006
1 Timothy		September–December 2003
2 Timothy		September–December 2004
Titus		May–August 2006
Philemon		May–August 2005
Hebrews		May–August 2008
James		January–April 2009
		May–August 2008
1 Peter		September–December 2008
2 Peter		January–April 2007
2, 3 John		September–December 2006
Revelation	1–3	May–August 2005

Subscribe...

Words of Life is published three times a year:
January–April, May–August and September–December.

Four easy ways to subscribe

- By post – simply complete and return the subscription form below
- By phone – +44 (0)20 7367 6580
- By email – mail_order@sp-s.co.uk
- Or pop into your local Christian bookshop

SUBSCRIPTION FORM

Name (Miss, Mrs, Ms, Mr)...

Address ....

....

.... Postcode ....

Tel. No..

Email* ....

Annual Subscription Rates
UK £10.50   *Non-UK* £10.50 + £3.90 P&P = **£14.40**
Please send me .... copy/copies of the next three issues of *Words of Life*
commencing with **May 2009**

Total: £ .... I enclose payment by cheque ☐
Please make cheques payable to *The Salvation Army*

Please debit my Access/Mastercard/Visa/American Express/Switch card

Card No. ☐☐☐☐ ☐☐☐☐ ☐☐☐☐ ☐☐☐☐   Expiry date: ___ /___

Security No. ☐☐☐ Issue number (Switch only) _____

Cardholder's signature: .... Date: ....

Please send this form and any cheques to: The Mail Order Department, Salvationist Publishing and Supplies, 66–78 Denington Road, Denington Industrial Estate, Wellingborough, Northamptonshire NN8 2QH, UK

☐ *We would like to keep in touch with you by placing you on our mailing list. If you would prefer not to receive correspondence from us, please tick this box. The Salvation Army does not sell or lease its mailing lists.